If a man does not keep pace
With his companions
Perhaps it's because
He hears a different drummer

Let him step
To the music HE hears
No matter how measured
Or far away

HENRY THOMAS THOREAU

Love ' n ' Light ' n ' Laughter

Paul

I

Previous books by Paul Bura

Mustn't Dent The Memory
Behind The Joker
From Under The Stairs
The Coming Of The Giants
The Space Between The Syllables
In The End Love Is All There Is
Joeb – Servant Of Gaia

The Oak On The Plain – (Honeytone Promotions)
Quest For Contact - (SB Publications)
The Drunk On The Train – (The Bosgo Press)
Brand New – (The Bosgo Press)

STEPPING
TO THE
DRUMMER
The Extraordinary Tales of a Psychic Man

foreword by Uri Geller

Beth Macnab,
Xmas 2002 1
(from Ma & Pa!!)

First published in 2000 by Honeytone Promotions
Newstead, Instow, North Devon, EX39 4LN

copyright © Paul Bura

Edited by Andy Thomas

Cover design by Hackersons. Hacker@zoom.co.uk.

Up to date photograph by Frank Youngs

Proof Reader: Beth Hay

ISBN: 0 9527924 2 7

Designed and printed by
W.O. Jones (Printers Ltd)
Llangefni, Angelsey.

Honeytone Promotions
01271 860653 FAX: 861373
Sandra@honeytone.co.uk.

CONTENTS

FOREWORD BY URI GELLER

Preface

FOREWORD

By URI GELLER

*T*his fascinating book comes from a man who *really* has a tale to tell. From his first mystical experience aged seven, just prior to catching polio, to a major back operation at 14 to try to rectify a crooked spine, to publishing his first book of poems and writing and performing his first play, aged 21, he has lived life to many extremes of pleasure and pain. He experienced mental agony as a result of a certain meditation technique ("I would have preferred my arms and legs to be torn off to be free of it") at 28. At 35, he woke up one morning and was unable to lift his arms as a result of Post-Polio Syndrome. These seven-year cycles continued until it was abruptly changed by a brain tumour, aged 52, "completely out of sequence", as he says. Through his brother Kevin, I was given the number of the hospital where he lay very ill, but the nurses wheeled his bed to the telephone and I was able to speak with him and give comfort and healing.

His life is full of psychic and spiritual events that will literally blow your mind. He tells of the early days when he trained as a medium with hilarious results, to the later years when he used to train budding mediums (or psychics) himself. He tells of his work amongst the Devic (or elemental) forces and his association with crop circles where he and others succeeded in bringing down a crop formation with the use of sound and visualisation. He tells of medicine wheels and their healing powers. He tells of the unseen team of workers, led by a being known as Joeb, that he works with and who, in his darkest hours, comforts him.

Always, his sense of humour comes shining through. He has learnt to laugh at himself (I too have had to do this) and not to take himself too seriously; "A song, a dance, a poem and a quick prophecy." He tells of his failures as well as his successes.

Somewhere in all of this, he became a writer, a voice-over artist, broadcaster and performing poet.

If I were to choose one tale which illustrated the rich and strange experiences this man has lived, it would be the Al Bowly story, where Paul attempted to communicate with a Big Band singer of the 1930s who was killed in the blitz, but 'came back' and made love to his former wife 40 years later. You have to read it to believe it!

Stepping to the Drummer, even by my standards, is an highly intriguing read. At times, you think he's making it all up. He isn't. Trust me, I'm a psychic.

URI GELLER   Sonning-on-Thames

PREFACE

*E*ver since I started writing and broadcasting poetry 25 years ago, the subject of the occult/paranormal/mysticism has tended to occur rather frequently in my work. Sometimes hidden, sometimes only hinted at.

The earlier chapters of *Stepping to the Drummer* are psychic and spiritual adventures that have gently (though not always) invaded my life since the age of seven. Some of the tales are quite bizarre and I make no excuse for them. They occurred in my life and I relate them here as best I can. The opening poem by H T Thoreau and his reference to "a distant drummer" is quite relevant, as you will see.

The later chapters of this book are a pulling together of these experiences in a new light. A sudden plunging head-first into the world of Sacred Site Guardians, Telluric earth energy lines, the being Jeuz from Sirius, my dear and close friend Joeb (from the Fifth Dimension) and the band of Lacota Indians who have shown me more in two years than I learned in the last 40! A world of crop circles and the Devic beings who assist in some of their creations. A world of medicine wheels and chakric energy. A world where dowsing is not just a tool, but a gateway to a mystical force, a gateway between this world and many others.

On August 12th 1995, I experienced the ceremony and ritual of *Lord Koot Hoomi's* (Kuthumi's) *staff* being placed into the Heart Chakra of the Earth's courier/ley system (lines of energy acting as givers and receivers of information), bringing in the higher healing power for the Earth Mother and all healers alike. This opened up lines of esoteric information that have, until now, been cut off from Mankind for many thousands of years.

But last, and by no means least, of these spiritual experiences is my awareness of the 'Ascension Process' itself, the reality, not just a 'New Age' idea, that the Earth's frequency is rising as surely as night follows day. Now is the time for us to wake up to who we REALLY are, where we have come from and where we are going. Time, as many of you have already noticed, is speeding up and NOT because of that old excuse of advancing years. Even the young are noticing it. The sun still rises and the sun still sets, there are still only 24 hours in a day, yet time is racing away. What's happening?

Come in number seven, your time is up!

PAUL BURA

CHAPTER 1

*H*ow dare they drag me away from my sun-drenched, sea-infested, care-free idle with the clatter and ding of penny arcades, the smell of hot 3-in-1 oil mingling with the odour of fried onions, hot-dogs, and the sea? How dare they?

Pop Prestley, "To me he was a god". To Pop's right are my grandmother and my little sister Melly, plus cats, Peter, Tiger and Jackie.

I was five and the State said that I should go to school. Go to school I went and there was no arguing. Never mind about my plans to be a fisherman with Pop Prestley. Looking back, he was my first teacher. He taught me how to bait a hook and fish! I was nuts about fishing. Pop owned a boat named *Seagull 11*. And on special, sun-sodden days he would take me with him. We would phut!-phut!-phut! out with the exhaust smell of paraffin and petrol making rainbows on the surface of the glassy sea. Away. Away. I had no thought for the 'morrow, I lived in the moment as all children do. And when Pop hauled in his lobster pots I would help him. He tied a piece of fish to a rope. I swear that I caught that mackerel and Pop hadn't put it on my line. I put it in an old tin to show mother and father (who owned a fish restaurant). Dad filleted it and cooked it for me. The sweetest fish I ever ate!

Pop swore that only he and I knew where the key was, the key to his shed where the smell of tar took your breath away, where lay hidden a treasure-trove of old nets and oars, fishing lines and rods, old fishing-reels made of wood and cat-gut! What would I have given for a reel of catgut! The key was in the gutter above the door. "Shhh, don't tell anyone," he said. And I never did.

Sometimes, though, we hauled up less savoury objects from the sea. One day, my friend Croyse White had been trying unsuccessfully to retrieve an object from the water with a stick. I watched him try and try again. It was bright yellow and had fins. No, not a fish. It was to cause quite a stink though. Croyse gave up. He walked dejectedly up the beach and out of sight. Now it was my chance to have a go at trying to possess it. At six years old, I was nobody's fool and, wearing my wellies, was able to get that much closer to it. I attached a piece of wire

My Grandfather. Now you know where I get my devastating good looks!

1

My Grandad went through two world wars as a sailor in the Royal Navy. Perhaps he thought the bomb was a dummy!

that I had found round one of the fins. At last I had it. I dragged it clear of the water and was just about to lift it up when my grandfather, taking a stroll along the beach after a session in the pub, wobbled down the beach to see what I had got. "I'll give you a hand, son." He slurred.

Now, my grandad had been in both world wars and you would have thought that it might just have entered his head that this thing resembled a bomb and would have sent various alarm-bells clanging. "Don't worry grandad, I can manage." With that, I heaved the 'bomb' up in both arms and carried it up the beach. Grandad, slightly unsteadily, followed me. I had to negotiate some very steep steps - and clang! - I rested the bomb on one step whilst I got up. Then clang again! I rested the bomb on the other step. There were three steps in all. I made my way the short distance to my father's restaurant The Oyster Bar with my grandad in tow. As I walked in the restaurant, I couldn't understand why people were hurling themselves at the doors and disappearing rather rapidly. I walked into the kitchen. There was a look of horror on my parents' face when I presented my trophy: "Now... er, put it down gently, son," said my father. "NO! not near the gas stoves!" He gave a sort of strangled cry and had trouble breathing. "Put it down GENTLY on the table AWAY from the ovens!" he urged gently but firmly. "There, that's it. Gently does it." I put my bomb carefully on the table indicated, whilst all hell broke loose. The police were called, together with the bomb squad!

A kindly policeman spoke to me about the dangers of 'things lying on the beach' and I, in future, was to "leave them alone". It turned out to be a Second World War flare. If it had gone off in that small space... well, it doesn't bear thinking about.

My grandfather? My grandmother saw to him!

It was 1950. My father took me to Gundolf House, Beltinge Hill, Herne Bay in Kent, a privately run school overseered by two elderly sisters, Miss Golding and Miss Daisy. He dropped me off in his shooting-brake car (you know, with genuine wood round the trim) and told me to "behave yourself, son, and do what the teachers tell you to do!" I remember taking an apple for lunch and leaving it behind in the car. I vividly recall Miss Daisy, a white-haired, pear-shaped matron of a woman, welcoming me and ushering me quietly into a large front room with a roaring fire where, lined up like pews, was a row of little desks. A walnut-wood piano stood there, with affixed brass candlesticks, at which was seated, in a bright floral dress, Miss Daisy's sister, Miss Golding.

Miss Golding was slightly larger and rounder than Miss Daisy, but not so fierce-looking. The room was jammed tight with children neatly lined up in their respective classes. I joined a row that I thought appropriate and was gently moved to another line by Miss Head, who was *my* teacher. We sang hymns and Miss Daisy took morning prayers. Then we all filed

out, except for Miss Golding's class who remained behind. I was shown into the next room and to my desk. I really couldn't help it, but I fell asleep! I was gently shaken about mid-morning

Miss Golding and Miss Daisy with all the pupils of their school, Gundolf House. Top row, 11th from left, Josie; middle row, 14th from left, me; front row, 6th from left, Melly.

where we were given milk in tiny, half-pint milk bottles with straws. All the children got out their biscuits and sandwiches and wot-not. It was then that I remembered my apple!

I got the love-bug pretty early. The first was a young student teacher who was as blonde as Marilyn Monroe and so pretty I couldn't drag my eyes away from her face. She was the daughter of a corner-shop owner who sold sweets and her name was Miss Watkins and she was just seventeen! I did heroic things for her like running so fast that my heels would kick my bum. She was most impressed: "Gosh I wish I could do that, Paul," she said, and swept off in a fragrant cloud of something-or-other.

But my real *first* love was just three-years-old. Her name was Mary. She was enchanting: the prettiest girl on Earth. She used to wait for me as I climbed Beltinge Hill on my way to school. I would give her presents, like an old coin and an exercise book (nicked from school - only the best for my girl) and a stub of a pencil so she could draw rings!

Gundolf House took in borders. It was there that I met Patricia. By now I was six and Mary no longer met me at her gate. I was going off her anyway. Patricia was the prettiest girl in the world.

Me, aged 4, with a waitress on the wall of the then Royal Hotel, opposite the Oyster Bar, a fish restaurant owned by my father and mother.

3

Grandma and us kids just before I caught Polio.

I would leap mighty cliffs at a single bound for her favours and jump down from the seafront onto the shingle below (I hurt my back in the attempt. But she never knew. I wouldn't admit to pain. Besides, she ignored me). Me and my mates, when she and the other borders went out in a crocodile-bunch, hauled with rope a great log under the burning sun. My mates, of course, wondered (but never knew) why I swaggered the most and preened myself, stripped to the waist and smeared with beach-tar, baring my chest, whipping the slaves with an imaginary whip. Wow, if they ever knew, I'd be in trouble. But Patricia remained unimpressed, an air of indifference surrounded her.

My next target was Janet: she was the prettiest girl on Earth and I would have given my life for just one kiss... then there was... and on and on and on. Never could I get close enough. My love life was hopeless, impossible.

In 1952, my seventh summer, we were packed off to my grandparents for the summer holiday with my little brother, Kevin, my sister Melly and elder sister, Josie. How dare they do this to us, how dare they! Being dragged away from the seaside that we loved and packed off to the country! It was BOR-ING! Mind you, with my parents in the fish restaurant trade it was the best thing... for them! Not having to put up with us kids running in and out: "Dad, where's my fishing rod?" Or: " Mum, can I have some chips?" "Can I have a milk-shake?" "Can I have some pennies for the arcade?" "Can I go for a boat trip?" "Ah, that's not fair, Kevin's got more sweets than I have." "Can I leave my lug-worms in the fridge?" "Ow, just 'cos Josie's older she can stay up later than us. *IT'S NOT FAIR!*" "It's *Wiley Price and his Orchestra* at the Bandstand. It's fancy-dress night. Can we dress up as pirates?" "Ahh, she's got more chips then me!" "Melly's cut her knee on the rocks, can I watch it bleed?" "If we're good, can we go to the pictures? It's Roy Rogers and Trigger! Ahh, go on pleeeease..." Perhaps they had a point.

It was during my seventh summer, in the country with my grandparents at Wigmore near Gillingham, Kent, that I had two experiences that literally changed my life. One was a purely

Wiley Price introduces me on wash-board and mouth organ, with Raymond Russel on plastic guitar. We played Green Door.

4

spiritual one (though I didn't know at the time) and one was of an entirely physical nature. In time, they became completely linked to the other. My first experience was, I now realise, completely spiritual. I rode my bike over to Bredhurst to the pub called The Bell. (A frequent visitor was my grandfather. Though he was only five-foot two he could put away 14 pints in one session... and still ride his bike home!) I rode my bike down a little lane beside the pub. I'm not sure what really happened but I remember thinking "this is all for me". The birds formed an avenue of sound that was directed at ME!

My mother aged 16: promotion picture for agents.

The sound was so beautiful that I got off my bike, thrust it against a grassy bank and sank down in the grass, the smell of which was the best anaesthetic I knew. Surely a god had wired this circuit. I can't remember if I slept or how long I lay there. But it was the first experience of feeling something outside of myself (or was it inside?), something greater than myself, something magical, mystical and wonderful. To hear not only that orchestra of birds, but also to feel a part of it, part also of the grassy bank itself! The sun began to dip behind the trees and I had to go home for tea! I didn't tell anybody. How could I? At this stage in my life there were no words to express it (nor today). "Anyhow," I told myself, "I just listened to the birds. What's so big a deal about that?" Yet it must have been, because I regard it still as my first spiritual experience.

Miss Daisy told the class something very interesting, well at least I thought it was interesting. As a young girl (I thought in my child-mind that she'd always been that old!) she stayed in a house that was reputedly haunted! When she "retired for the night" – her words not mine – she was about to go to sleep when all of a sudden she could hear children laughing and chattering. She could actually *feel* the children as they clambered and played on the bed. Then it stopped as suddenly as it started! When she came downstairs for breakfast she mentioned it. Apparently the room was once a playroom for children. I was too young to ask questions like "what happened to the children?". But her explanation was that the sound must have got "trapped in the chimney" and played back in some mysterious way. She didn't explain, however, the fact that she could *feel* them as they jumped on and off the bed! That was to be my first introduction to the so-called paranormal.

And the second experience? A purely physical one: I caught polio from a stagnant pool in my grandmother's front garden. The bungalow had been let to a young couple with a baby and they had only just got it back. She and grandad were about to fill in the pool. My grandparents never forgave themselves. Me? I just waited it out, determined that I would return to the seaside that I loved and carry on where I left off. Bravery had nothing to do with it. As a kid you take it in your stride. My mother recently told me that when I was in St Barts hospital, Chatham, I said to her that the reason I had caught polio was so the doctors could study me and find out about this thing called polio! On hearing the news that I might die, my mother's hair turned white overnight and my father went down into the cellar below our restaurant and sobbed his heart out.

Me in my first spinal jacket. Note the way it keeps me to attention.

Coming from a family of entertainers - my mother was a variety dancer from

Bob Bura of Bura and Hardwick animations-(Camberwick Green; Trumpton)-at some time during his acting days.

the age of 14, my father was a professional wrestler - it was not exactly out of the ordinary to want to be a part of that seemingly wonderful world. I wanted to be an actor, a dancer, an impressionist, and a multiple instrument musician. My uncle Bob (Bob Bura of Bura and Hardwick Animations: *Camberwick Green, Trumpton*, and many others) was a child entertainer singing and dancing in night-clubs from a very early age, then graduating to ventriloquism and puppetry. Polio, it seemed, put an end to all that – but not so.

Catching polio was the one great important feature of my life. It taught me patience, it made me sit still for once in my life and observe it, observe what was going on, what was *really* going on. I could go into detail about the various hospital-schools that I attended after I caught polio. How I took my first steps with my calliper and spinal-jacket (I swear that I was pushed by unseen hands towards the arms of a waiting

St. Bart's Hospital, Chatham, just after being released from the Iron Lung.

doctor). How I kissed my first nurse at eight-years-old (Nurse Roberts. I remember her to this day). When I tried innocently to kiss her lips, working my way round from her cheek, she suddenly stopped me. "Oh no," she said. "That's where my boyfriend kisses me!" I was aghast. Boyfriend? Boyfriend? What about me? I was outraged, not to mention jealous.

I decided that I didn't like school... and I never would. I liked the activities outside of school. But learning? Strictly for the birds, man. Little did I know that later in

Nurse Roberts, left. I was devastated when I discovered she had a boyfriend. (Cheyney Hospital).

my life I was to become a poet and writer and that learning how to spell was of the greatest importance. Thank god for dictionaries and, later on, the spell-checker!

Chailey Heritage in East Sussex was a hell-hole that I would never forget, here best described in my poem of the same name:

CHAILEY HERITAGE

We ate shepherds pie
On the journey to Sussex.
Even then I couldn't really believe
That they would leave me.

"This school is a special school
Where there are children like you!"

To me there was no difference
Between normal people and the crippled ones,
They were all children.

When we arrived
I knew that they would go,
That I would remain behind.

I was fitted out with short trousers
And heavy studded boots that made
My legs feel weak.
We didn't have coats
But were given cloaks and striped shirts.

On Sundays we were given Harris Tweed jackets
And grey flannels.

"He's not going to be very warm in these"
Said my mother to my father,
Who made jokes to make me feel better.

I watched them drive away.
I cried because that was
The only expression I had.
I wanted to blame them for leaving me
But I knew how much it hurt them.
I could see the pain in their eyes.

I was bullied and beaten up
From time to time.
I wasn't used to violence.
In this place it was the law of the jungle:
Kill or be killed!
I died many times
But I got used to dying.

I remember a big boy that used to spit
Full in my face whenever he saw me:
He'd wait round corners then jump
Out at me.
There was nothing I could do about it,
He was much faster than I.
(He was eventually expelled from the school
for excessive violence.
He was a cripple.)

I remember being held down
With metal chairs whilst my legs
Were stung with stinging nettles.

I still stared at the empty driveway
Waiting for that familiar car
Carrying my mummy and daddy.
I soon learned to say 'Mum and Dad'
'Cos 'Mummy and Daddy' was 'posh talk'.
I was blackmailed
Into lending my sheath knife
To a boy with no fingers.
I never got it back.

I was persecuted by a boy named Snelling
Whose rubber-like legs were encased in steel,
He knew my Achilles-heel:
My fear of falling over.
He would prod me with his crutches.

I made friends with a boy
Who had one finger where his arm
Should have been
His other shoulder
Supported an artificial limb
That didn't work.
He wrote beautifully
With a fountain-pen
And was a wizard at Ping-Pong.

I learned a lot too:
How to swear!
How to fight!
How to get out of a bath, unaided.
I'll say one thing though:
The food was terrific!

Years later, the late *Ian Dury* of *Ian Dury and the Blockheads* fame (a polio boy who went to the same school) said of this poem: "That's what it was really like. This geezer tells it like it was!" Mind you, when I finally met him I said to him, jokingly, mind, "You're not the bastard who used to beat me up, are you?" "No I'm f***ing well not!" he said, and limped off in a huff. I tried to explain that I was joking, but he wasn't having any of it. Sensitive soul.

As the poem says, during my stay at Chailey Heritage the only thing that kept me going was the prospect of the excellent food. For instance, never had I *tasted* cheese cutlets like it, before or since.

It took me about three weeks of intensive homesickness to settle down to that barbaric and cruel regimen, barbaric because the inmates were mixed with psychopaths and sadists. It was like *Tom Brown's Schooldays* where you became victimized. It was the law of the jungle: kill or be killed!

I knew that they had got my mate John Bailey because I could hear his screams. They had him in the corner of the dormitory. He was half-naked and they were beating him with pillows. But then I could see that this was merely a distraction; what really made him scream was that they were beating his deformed, naked feet with boots, the heavy boots that were the standard issue! I was his friend, his only friend. We used to keep each other company during those bleak days. Even then they would 'get him', smashing a metal crutch across his face, nose splitting, blood splashing all over me. And still I did nothing, only comfort him. I was paralysed with fear. Sneaking (telling) was not allowed, you see. And there he was again confronted by his demons, surrounded by his tormentors. "Bura, come and see what we're doing to your friend" the head demon called out (I don't remember his name, but he was later expelled). My legs turned to jelly. I got down onto the bed, then lowered myself onto the floor and underneath the beds; bed by bed I dragged myself along the slippery floor until I was under the bed where they had him cornered. Trying to dodge the blows, John tried to defend himself. Two or three of the demons were on the floor also, beating his bare feet. "Come on, Bura," they said, "or you'll get it too!" There was a spare boot... I lifted it... and brought it down softly on his feet. "Harder, Bura," they said, "harder!..." Then the master came in and they scuttled away like rats.

I tried to tell him, as he sobbed his heart out on the bed, that I was only trying to stop them. He called for his mother from time to time, thinking perhaps that she had abandoned him in some way. I thought that too, I thought that I was abandoned, but what I didn't know then was that my parents had done it out of pure love and concern for my welfare, as indeed his had. I don't know whether John believed me or not that I was trying to stop them; to this day I really don't know. We remained pals, but it was never the same.

When I finally did go home to my seaside the following summer, I just carried on as if nothing had happened. I had a plastic spinal-jacket and calliper, but even the calliper was discarded after a couple of years with the help and dedication of my family. In time, I formed my own 'gang', complete with flags, and terrorised the locals with as much style as I could muster. After all, I was in a wheelchair. I used to be wheeled around Woolworths and drop stink-bombs in front of me. As they went under the chair, my cousin Alan, who was pushing me, would tread on these little glass phials, shattering to release the evil-smelling liquid inside. We stood outside and waited. They came pouring out, handkerchiefs clutched to their noses. Harry the mechanic from Harris's garage suffered the same fate. We'd throw them in the pit whilst he was working under a car and then shoot off, wheelchair flying! He still remembers it to this day: "You were a right little f***er" he'd say, smiling in his soft Kentish accent. Well, at nine-years-old you've *got* to do it, haven't you?

Like Richmal Crompton's *Just William* books, my gang and I scowled and raked our way around Herne Bay, full to the brim with self-importance, fighting foes limited only by our imagination. My wheelchair became the envy of many a rival, 'fixed-wheeled' though it was. But then I triumphed yet again! I acquired a tricycle! Not *any* old tricycle, but a purpose-built tricycle made by the Norman factory in Middlesex. Now I was cooking; now I had freedom; now I could choose wherever I wanted to go. Not only that, but I could crowd my little brother and sister on the back-axle and shoot down Beltinge Hill at a fair old kick. Herne Bay was my oyster... and the world? Wow, here I come!

It was a beautiful, summer's day and we had just come out of school. As usual, my little brother Kevin and my sister Melly (who had taken on the job of pushing me up the steep hill) clambered on the back of my tricycle on our way home. I decided that we should go the Downs route, which ran parallel to Beltinge Hill and was the quickest way to the sea. I let go of the brakes and we gathered speed. In the distance, I could see a car descending the hill. By now we had gathered enough speed and were gaining on the car - not only were we gaining on the car, but we were going FASTER than the car! Either I could brake or overtake!

The driver of the car must have seen us in his rear mirror. The look of sheer horror on his face when we pulled out to overtake is indelibly printed on my memory. A large kid on a tricycle with two screaming kids welded on the back was overtaking him. He could not believe his eyes! It was a split second decision and we went for it. Never mind about the danger, never mind that I had responsibility for my brother and sister. The prospect was irresistible, irresistibly irresistible! In that delicious moment we could have conquered the world and stolen its oyster, pearl and all.

It was about this time that I experienced my first taste of spiritualism. I didn't know what it meant any more than I knew what a spiritual healer was, but my parents were prepared to allow me to try anything that might help me. So just once a week Jess Mount, a local fisherman and pleasure-boat owner, and the brother-in-law of my hero Pop Prestley, and his wife wheeled me to the local Christian Spiritualist Church for a healing session with Mr Hughes. I really didn't know what was going on. Here was this bloke washing his hands, muttering prayers, kneeling in front of me with his eyes closed and running his hands over the most affected parts of my body. What was he doing? I remember that his hands always smelt of soap and that he had a Welsh accent.

Me and Howard Thing on that tricycle.

Sometimes Jess and his wife would take me to a Spiritualist Meeting and I would watch someone called a 'medium' talk in a strange voice with his or her eyes closed telling people strange things about Red Indian and Chinese 'guides' and people who had passed over the veil. None of it meant much to me but I have to say I was fascinated, even if I didn't understand what the hell was going on. Whether the healing helped I'm not sure, but I did improve a little. This of course could have been due to all the swimming I did. Nobody could keep me out of the water. I was equal to anyone in the sea. I mean the sea wasn't exercise, was it? I hated the word exercise. Who wanted to exercise? There was a big world out there and I wanted to get at it. I didn't want to exercise. But swimming was different, swimming was fun. Swimming made me part of the sea I loved. The sea was powerful. Water was powerful – salt or otherwise.

When I was about 12, my folks took me to see a famous healer, Harry Edwards. The procedure was that one of Mr Edward's helpers would call out to the audience "Is there anyone here suffering from eye problems?" Dozens of hands would shoot up. People would scream for attention. "Is there anyone suffering from rheumatism?" Again mayhem would break out. Out of all the hands mechanically waving someone would be picked out. They would climb up on to the stage where they were suddenly surrounded by a scrum of white coated healers including, of course, the governor himself, Harry Edwards. Someone held a microphone for him

12

while he told the audience what the patient's problem was and how he and his fellow healers could help with the power of God.

I saw a lady whose fingers were badly stiffened from arthritis. Harry took her fingers and gently rotated them. There appeared to be no pain. Within minutes she was clenching and unclenching her hands, something she apparently had not done for years. I saw a woman with a humpback have it straightened before the gaze of hundreds. I was very impressed. Another had the sight restored to one of her eyes – how much sight I could not remember.

Then suddenly the shout went up for people with spinal problems. My father's hand shot up. The people with us, I can't remember who they were, started waving and shouting. Before I knew what was happening I was being half-carried down the aisle toward the stage. I was helped very rapidly up the stairs and was seated in full view of the audience. Harry Edwards was plumpish, white-haired and pink, with very warm hands. His sleeves rolled up, he seemed preoccupied, with what I didn't know. He felt my back and then asked my father to remove my spinal brace. So off came my jacket and shirt revealing my new leather and steel spinal support. I felt a bit of a berk sitting there half-naked in front of this wild audience of hopefuls. Harry spoke into the microphone: "This boy has a double curvature of the spine. I am now going to attempt to straighten it." The crowd roared.

He ran his fingers down my spine while his fellow healers rubbed my legs. With a jerk of his fingers he pulled against my spine! "It is now straight!" The crowd roared again. "We will now get him to walk without the aid of his support." The crowd went barmy. Little did they or Harry Edwards know that I could walk without it anyway. I stood up and was asked to walk, leaning on my Dad, across the stage. The audience went berserk and I felt wonderful. It didn't matter that I could walk without the jacket, it was the knowledge that my spine was straight, really straight. I could not wait to get home and show my Mum, sisters and brother. When I got home I lay down on my bed and took my vest off. I called my Dad in. "Well, Dad, is it straight? Is it?" My Dad looked, he paused, his face remained impassive. "Yes son, it's straight, it's straight." He quietly left the room. I knew that it wasn't. I knew that he was lying, but it didn't matter, it didn't matter. I always knew I had to be this way. I am not sure how I knew, but I did. It was not, on reflection, karmically possibly for me to be healed. Improved, yes, but not completely healed.

It took me years to understand the laws of cause and effect, action and reaction, but now it makes perfect sense. Many, though, would consider it a cop-out, a way of explaining why it is that so many people suffer so horribly and others seem to live a long and seemingly pain-free life. But unless you accept that eternity is *here* and not in some far away place, unless you accept that life does not end here, but it is eternal *now*, then, of course, the idea of karma will remain just balls. How can I prove that life is continuous? I can't. But I hope that my seven-year cycles of experience, the major events in my life that always fall every seven years, joined together with some pretty wild paranormal and spiritual experiences, will at least give you some idea of why I think the way I do.

CHAPTER 2

When I was 14, I had to go into hospital for a major back operation. Mr Strange (and believe me there was nothing strange about this man) decided that a spinal fusion, the fusing together of the lower part of my spine by taking bone from my hip, would help straighten my back. Obviously, it would take many operations to straighten it completely. A plaster bed was constructed for me to lie on after the operation. The bed, made from plaster of Paris, was full length with a top and a bottom. Each half was fitted to a half-wheel which in turn was attached to a metal frame which lay on a bed. The idea was that if I were lying on my back and needed to be turned over, the nurse would lift the half on top of me, fixing one side of the attached half-wheel to the bottom half-wheel. This was then clamped together and I was rotated like a chicken on a spit.

The operation was the worst physical pain that I have ever experienced. It was so bad I nearly blacked out with the sheer agony. But over the weeks the pain gradually subsided and I settled into yet another hospital way of life. Because I was rather old for my age, I was put in the men's ward where sessions of dirty jokes were the norm and post 'lights out' farting left me helpless with laughter. Listening to Tony Hancock and to *Spike* and *The Goon Show* sharpened my sense of humour and made life much more tolerable.

I knew that my mother and father were going through a bad patch. My father had an operation to remove an ulcer. A clot of blood went to his brain and he lost the feelings of his left arm and the side of his face. For a while he suffered fits. Dad was always a very athletic person and this was a terrible blow to him. It resulted in his turning to drink. Coupled with the drugs he was having to take, this caused a personality change. He was fine if he stayed off the booze but he was not my Dad when he was drunk. I dreaded him visiting me in hospital because he was nearly always drunk and it was very obvious to everyone, except Dad, that he had had a few.

It was around this time that I started to write short stories. I had a pretty fertile imagination and I needed to express it, but the writing ended there – for the time being.

The operation did not exactly gear me into thinking of ethereal things, but something was stirring, something was beckoning to me. I had no idea what.

After six months I came home. I was 15 now and, thank God, I had left school. I never really liked school very much, at least not the learning aspect. I was just lazy. As I've already said, most of my education was taught in hospitals and schools for the disabled. I never passed any exams because I never took any. But the best time I had at school was at Herne Bay Secondary Modern, mainly because I was made a librarian which gave me a certain sense of power, but also I could indulge myself with reading. I won the school talent competition playing the mouth organ with a school mate of mine (I think his name was Roger Hext) and for playing a sea captain in the school play *Over the Rainbow* (or was it *The Rainbow's End?*). Anyway, creativity was beginning to enter my life. I was only at Greenhill for about nine months but I kissed my first girl properly there behind the stage during a break in rehearsals for the talent competition, so I can honestly say I enjoyed it.

John Hardwick and my sister Josie at Pinewood Studios

When I was 16 I went to a Rehabilitation Unit in Croydon to learn some sort of trade. I stayed in a YMCA and had to walk quite a distance to catch a bus each day to the centre, but each day got easier and I became fitter than I had ever been in my life. I had to keep stopping to recharge the body, but nevertheless I was in pretty good shape. They tried me first at gents hairdressing, but I couldn't handle the standing. Then they tried me at scientific glass-blowing, but my right arm kept giving way with the strain and I ended up with bent glass.

In desperation, they shoved me into a workshop where I learnt to operate lathes of every shape and size churning out nuts and bolts and other mind-numbing items. People by now were beginning to fascinate me. I would listen very closely to stories that the older blokes would tell, especially those associated with the supernatural, those which had no logical explanation. I asked questions that nobody could answer. If you experience these strange things why can't I? What is a ghost anyway? If God was supposed to have created everything, who created God? Etcetera.

I left the centre after three months with the recommendation that I might be useful in an office. An office – me! – only fit to work in an office!? Never! I swore I would never do that. Never! There had to be something else.

It was about this time that a TV programme, *One Step Beyond*, was being screened. Such a programme of apparently true supernatural stories was fuel to my frantic imagination. They seemed to confirm much that seemed totally real to me. I knew all this stuff of second sight, teleportation, prophecy and visions was all possible. They may not have been exactly everyday events for 99% of people, but they existed. I knew that they did. I had to find out more. By this time my parent's marriage was nearing its end. My father had an affair with a lady and made her pregnant. My mother immediately filed for divorce.

The restaurant was let out by my father for a ridiculous sum and we all moved to a place called *The Tudor*, a pub and dance hall on the sea front at Herne Bay that my father was running. Eventually my father was made bankrupt regardless of my mother's superhuman efforts to make the restaurant pay (prior to my father letting it). My sister Josie and I fought a losing battle to keep the pub open. We did manage to pull it round by holding live rock dances but a terrible winter wrecked the ancient heating system and everything folded. We moved to a rented house in Spencer Road.

By now I was reading everything I could lay my hands on that could fill this empty void within me. Books by the Rev. Stainton Moses gripped me and, like so many people then, the books by Lobsang Rampa thrilled me more than I could say, even though at 16 years old I was still a little dubious. I was also visiting my local Spiritualist Church about twice a week, listening very hard to what the mediums had to say. I had more than my fair share of messages. Some were puerile rubbish, some were worth mentally storing away for future reference, and some were very exact indeed, which brings me to the first experience that actually rocked our family with its accuracy.

A couple of summers before my father went bankrupt, I was serving behind the counter in the restaurant when a man and woman came in for fish and chips. My mother served them and carried on as usual with the other customers. I was not feeling very well, a slight headache, but it was nothing serious. Suddenly the woman looked at me and told me that I had a headache and should lie down. Then she turned to my mother and asked where the grey-haired lady was who used to work here. My mother thought she was referring to Mrs Packman who used to cook and wash up for us. But the woman said no, the lady in question was tallish and rather largely built. My mother said that the description was of her mother who had died a few months ago. The woman

The psychic lady and her husband walked into our restaurant and asked where the tall lady with grey hair was. My Grandmother. She had a message from her for my mother!

17

My brother Kevin. The dog at his feet is Shadow: "Shadow no longer responded to our telepathic calling."

said that this was the lady to whom she referred and that she had a message from her for my mother. My mother was openly shocked and certainly stuck for words.

The lady proceeded to tell her that her son (me) had caught the polio virus from a stagnant pond in her mother's front garden. She went on to say that she had always felt guilty about it, but was now able to help him (me) much more now that she had passed than ever she could during her life here. My mother was dumbfounded.

You see, a couple of months prior to my grandmother's death my mother was standing beneath the cherry tree in my grandmother's garden (apparently they were talking about the damage the squirrels had wrought with the fruit) when my grandmother asked my mother what she thought of spiritualism. My mother replied that in her opinion people should not try to get in touch with the spirits of the dead, but that, if anything, it should be the dead that contact the living. And that is how the conversation ended, but now my grandmother had done just that – she had contacted the living, my mother, from the other side. To me all this seemed perfectly natural, very exciting and a little scary, but perfectly natural.

During our stay in Spencer Road I carried out experiments with telepathy using our dog, Shadow. On two occasions Shadow had been out all day and the whole family were very worried. I suggested that we all sit down and concentrate our minds on Shadow, mentally calling him home. Within two minutes the familiar sound of Shadow hurtling over the garden fence shattered the silence. He raced into the kitchen, tail going like a propeller. He was promptly sick, bringing up fresh meat that he had obviously just been eating from somewhere when he received our call. Coincidence?

A few weeks later the same thing happened. This time, however, he wasn't sick. Not long after these experiments, Shadow was killed in a freak accident. No amount of our telepathic calling brought him home. A few days later he was found in a warehouse; a packing case had apparently fallen on him. He had been unwell a day or two before. My brother, Kevin, whose dog it was, was heartbroken. Some months later Kevin developed a fever, some sort of viral infection. During this period he became mildly delirious. Afterwards Kevin told us that Shadow had come to him and licked his face.

There are many recorded cases of delirium allowing the spirit body a greater sense of freedom, opening the door of consciousness between the physical and the ethereal mind without the usual method of memory erasal coming into play. Memory erasal is most common during the sleep state, though some of us are better at recall of dream experience than others. People undergoing operations or indeed dental surgery, anything where a general anaesthetic is used, find that out-of-the-body experiences are extremely vivid and the memory stays with them forever. Folk using lysergic acid (LSD), mescaline or other hallucinogenic drugs have had similar experiences. The difference being that usually the drug is in control of the user instead of the other way round. In other words, the drug gate-crashes the mind, forcing open the doors of consciousness and sometimes causing great distress to the user experiencing events that he is not in a position to control, let alone understand. Instead of tuning into one wavelength at a time, he is tuning into many. The resulting confusion can sometimes drive you insane.

My visits to the Spiritual Church gave me much food for thought, but it wasn't just psychic phenomena and proof of survival that interested me. I realised that anyone could develop their psychic senses, but it didn't necessarily bring them closer to God. Whether good or bad we will all survive death so spiritualism in my view can prove survival and that is its prime function. I was appalled at the people I met who considered that they were great spiritual beings simply because they had the gift of clairvoyance or healing. Even at the age of 17 I was beginning to realise how gullible folk can be when it comes to psychic matters. Mind you, my own youth and emotional immaturity were just as susceptible to deception if I really got carried away. It was the silent communion with the spirit that I needed. The tuning in to the great consciousness, the great silence, the infinite, the higher part of myself, was what I needed to understand.

CHAPTER 3

*B*y now, I was a familiar figure at our local Spiritualist Church and messages for my spiritual well-being were coming thick and fast. At times I wondered whether it was my youth and obvious disability that drew the mediums to me. I was told that I had a main guide called Omid Elebdah. A picture of him by someone called Tuff showed him to be Arabic.

One evening, a particular medium was giving a very inspired address delivered with great passion. Every word he uttered seemed to make perfect personal sense to me. Over and above that, he seemed actually to be talking directly at me even though his eyes were closed. I cannot remember exactly what he said, but it was a very clear summary of all that I had held dear and what had happened in my life, my longings and desires right up to that particular point in time. Later, as usual, the medium gave his demonstration of clairvoyance. When he came to me he told me that it was necessary for me to develop my psychic senses in order for me to carry out certain work in the future; that in the near future I would be asked to join a developing circle.

To develop my psychic senses was something I had always wanted to do, but this sort of message was common enough. As I was about to leave the church, two ladies approached me. They told me that they had been thinking of asking me to join their developing circle after hearing various messages that I had received over the months and that they had told no-one of this, let alone the medium whose message I had just received. I was astounded and delighted and gladly accepted their offer. This was the start of a very happy period for me. Once a week I would sit with a lovely group of ladies headed by a very fine medium called Eileen Newport. Most of the ladies were in their late fifties (or so it seemed to me – when you are 18 anyone over 40 is knocking on a bit) so I really was just the lad.

They all treated me very kindly and answered as best they could my eager questions. After a few months I started to develop rather rapidly my first personal experience of the strange. Strange only because nothing quite like it had ever happened to me before. After the opening prayers we settled down into the silence. Faint background music was played on a small tape recorder (paid for by a sub of half-a-crown a week per sitter - 12p). Incense burned and the room was beautifully warm, everything designed to help in relaxation. I cleared my head as instructed and then started to gently look at the now blank screen of my mind. The usual swirling mind-clouds were visible, but that was all. Then suddenly I felt my body beginning to tingle, my breathing became firm and rhythmic. I relaxed down in my chair almost in a slump.

I was not sure what was taking place and was not at all sure what the hell I should do! I was not, however, at all frightened. By now, the other sitters had become aware of something happening and Eileen knelt in front of me and took my hands. I had this overwhelming desire to speak. I wasn't sure, but I felt that I, or someone close to me, invisibly close that is, was trying desperately to communicate. At this point Eileen started to ask, very gently, "Is there anybody there?" Well, this question was so typical of the phrase that spiritualists use that, even though I was in what was termed 'a light trance', it caused me to splutter and inwardly scream with laughter. It was at this point that I felt I ought to say something, anything. This was my mistake. I tried to mumble something and as I did, whoever it was who was trying to use me as a medium slipped away.

It was with some difficulty that I tried to gain some semblance of normality. I started to shake with cold. I was so cold that my teeth chattered! The room, I knew, was very warm, but I was so cold. A blanket was brought by one of the ladies and put around my shoulders. My first experience of psychic cold. After a cup of tea I tried to answer eager questions from my fellow sitters. By now I was getting somewhat warmer. I explained as best I could that someone was trying to speak through me, but who, I did not know. Eileen explained that I had now made the breakthrough, but I had tried too hard to speak and should be more patient and let whoever it was trying to communicate take their time.

From that moment on my psychic self became more aware, more finely tuned, but it was so subtle that sometimes I was not aware that I was seeing clairvoyantly. For example, if I were to ask you, the reader, to picture in your mind say – a rose – fairly easy huh? Okay, well that's how I see. Not in brilliant colour, not in sharply defined pictures, not in mind-blowing images. When I tune into my psychic self in order to see, I clear my mind then watch to see what thought pictures imprint themselves on my screen. The trick is to be able to tell what are ordinary everyday thought images and what are clairvoyant images. In my case, if I am 'seeing' it is usually preceded by what I describe as a psychic tingle, though not always. Of course, many people are gifted to the extent that they see as clearly as if watching colour TV. Although I see in rather grey mind images, I am also aware of colour: that is, although I am not *seeing* in colour I am experiencing it, and often very accurately.

Over the years, my mediumistic gift gradually gathered strength. It was during my own Family Circle that my teacher and guide at that time 'came through' properly and he spoke for the first time. After that, from time to time I was called on to use this gift, but I was, and am still, not entirely happy with it mainly because my own emotions can so easily play a part in whatever message is being transmitted. This is one reason why

I usually refuse to give clairvoyance to anybody who I am emotionally close to or who I know very well unless it comes spontaneously or unconsciously. Unconscious clairvoyance can be the most accurate.

For example, I remember meeting an old friend of mine whom I hadn't seen for a few years. I told him how good it was to see him again and that I was surprised he had given up his job as a golf professional to sell insurance. He looked at me blankly and shook his head. He was still a golf professional and had never sold insurance. We met again two years later. He looked at me a moment and then told me that since our last meeting he had been forced to give up golf as he couldn't earn enough and was now selling insurance. To me, at the time of this example of unconscious clairvoyance, I just knew and took for granted that he sold insurance. There was no way of my knowing that this was not a fact of that moment, but of two years hence,

This also brings to mind an example of psychometry (the ability to receive clairvoyant information, past, present and future, by touching or holding an object) that made me gasp with its accuracy. I had gone over to Canterbury to see my sister Josie who was living in Salisbury Road at the time. When I arrived, I was introduced to Peter Helm, a musician friend of my then brother-in-law who was giving this particular musician some extra music tuition. Josie told me that Peter was psychic, which is always a good opener for conversation. It turned out that Peter had a clairvoyant gift which was somewhat out of control. He would find himself being drawn, as if by a magnet, to certain places that in fact gave him the creeps. It seems that there was nothing he could do about it (I had the strong impression that this was a result of past-life psychic misuse). However, we got to talking and swapped a few experiences.

We decided that we would take the other's ring, write down whatever information we received and meet a week later. This we did and again met at Josie's place and exchanged pieces of paper. Peter wrote that he believed I had something to do with poetry (I was, and am, a writing and performing poet); that I was going through a particularly emotional crisis at the time (I had just got over a love affair); also that I wrote songs and sang (true, though very badly). There were other bits and pieces that he couldn't possibly have known. Remember, we had never met

Me reciting poetry on T.V.

23

before. He was, in all, about 50% accurate which is a pretty high score for clairvoyance.

Now it was my turn. I told Peter a few odd pieces of information which were pretty average; then I told him that his wife was pregnant, that she would have a son who would be born with a birth mark over his right eye. Peter looked at me for a moment, obviously shaken. Then he told me that nobody but he and his wife knew that she was pregnant. Six months later, Peter's wife gave birth to a boy. The doctor had to use forceps which left marks all over the little mite's forehead. All the marks disappeared rapidly within a few days except for one mark over his right eye that remained for over a week. When I heard that information it burst upon me with such certainty that I couldn't write it down quick enough. Its accuracy literally stunned me.

Perhaps at this juncture I should say that I am not, and never was, a spiritualist. I got involved with spiritualism simply because it gave me a few answers, apart from proving survival beyond this life, that I believe I could not have got elsewhere. Developing one's psychic gifts (and almost anyone can do it) does not necessarily bring you closer to God. The great Dutch clairvoyant, Croiset, was not a religious man, but he had an outstanding gift of clairvoyance, helping police uncover information that could never have been found by normal police procedure and he brought to justice many a murderer and law breaker. He found bodies that nobody else could find and found valuable objects thought to be lost forever.

I was asked many times to join the church, but I refused and have been a non-joiner of most things, religious and otherwise, most of my life. The only thing I ever joined was the Cubs (though I was a Samaritan for nine years). My small gift as a medium was sometimes called into play with dramatic results.

Many years ago in London, my sister Mellie (who, like me, finds the whole subject of the paranormal fascinating) asked me whether I would hold a séance for a young Turkish conductor of music who was working in London. He had heard that his father had just died and was unable to go to the funeral. He wanted desperately to contact his father, but was at the same time very sceptical. The bond between the Turkish father and son was very strong. I agreed to hold a sitting with the conductor, his lady at the time, my sister Mellie, and her husband Frank. I put on a recording of *Fantasia on a Theme* by Thomas Tallis, a piece of music which never fails to break down the barriers of my resistance and tunes me in. I then opened with a prayer. After what seemed only a short while I began to feel the personality of someone overshadowing me. The personality was strong and very emotional. I was almost certain it was the conductor's father but I could not be absolutely sure.

I remember this personality telling the rather sceptical conductor of music that he was so glad to meet his son once more before his final journey. He told his son how much he loved him, how much he loved his family, but it was time now for him to do other things in other places. The father was by now in tears and real tears were coursing down my cheeks, for I felt everything that the personality felt, yet still remained objective, a participating observer. The personality put out his hand towards his son and the son, now crying, took his father's hands "Don't go father, please don't go, not yet." By now, I was convinced that the personality was indeed the conductor's father. "I have to go now my son. I feel the pain too, but I must go." The son wouldn't let go of my/his father's hands and was deeply upset. I felt the personality beginning to slip away. Still the son held my hands. "Goodbye father, goodbye. I love you too." My hand went limp. The conductor let go of my hands and wiped his tears away. The whole group, seated round in a circle, were all in tears.

I waited until my body began running its normal course again. After some questioning, I found that I had, in fact (I only vaguely remember), described the conductor's father in some detail and it was this which made him realise that this was his father and by the end of the sitting there was no doubt in his mind. He had met and spoken to his father who had only died a week before. He was convinced of that, but I was very disappointed. Disappointed to find out that his father only had one leg. Why didn't I pick that up? It was valuable information and I was very angry and disappointed with myself for not knowing this. I knew that it was only his physical leg that he had lost and now that he had thrown off his physical body he would now be completely whole, but past experience had taught me that details like this are usually given or, in my case, experienced. Still the conductor made the contact he had come for and although moved to tears he went away a happier and more fulfilled person. He was able to say goodbye.

One thing I was always told was that one should never receive money in exchange for psychic or spiritual gifts. They should always be given freely. If one were to ask for money those gifts would be taken away. However, some mediums actually make a living out of their gifts, and I see nothing wrong in that unless you are a cheat. After all, a gift is a gift whether you be a painter, musician, writer or whatever. We all have to live. I remember a rather lean time for me when I put an ad in the local newspaper to do postal clairvoyant readings. I would ask the recipient to hold a fresh paper tissue that nobody else had touched, then seal it in an envelope, put it inside another envelope, and send it to me together with an SAE and £1. Thus for a few months I earned a few extra quid doing readings. At first I felt guilty, but then reasoned that I had done dozens of reading for free in my life, and many more since, and that I was giving good value for money. Even to this day I get the odd request from people for whom I did readings years ago to do a further reading. I usually refuse.

One interesting reading was seeing one particular gentleman fall down an open beer cellar trapdoor in the pavement. He wrote me a year later, to say, rather foolishly, that he was now recovering from such a fall.

CHAPTER 4

*I*n 1965, when I was 21, I wrote my first play, a comedy. My life-long friend Peter McKay read the first act, thought it was very funny (as it was written around our own personal idiosyncrasies) and suggested I finish it, which I did. We decided to produce and star in the play called *The Script Writers* and put it on at the local Beltinge Memorial Hall. My brother-in-law, Barry Cole, wrote a score for it and gathered a bunch of jazz musicians together for this one-off extravaganza. The play was a terrific local success (I wrote small cameo roles for my brother Kevin, and sisters Mellie and Josie). It was one of the happiest periods of my life and certainly one of the funniest. Peter and I started ad-libbing. The audience went wild. We could do no wrong. We threw in impressions, gags and spontaneous visual humour, humour that to Peter and I was second nature. Even the musicians were falling off the stand with mirth. If you can make musicians laugh - because they have seen it all - then you have cracked it.

Seated in the audience was Peter Flanders, father of Michael Flanders, of Flanders and Swann fame. He wrote to Southern Television and as a result we were asked to compose some satirical verse to the tune of *Three Blind Mice* (with me on piano) for youth; mods, rockers and the like. Thus we made our first TV appearance, then sat back and waited for offers to pour in. Nothing happened. We couldn't understand it. We had been on TV. Surely that made you an instant star! How bloody wrong and naïve can you get? We weren't that good – we thought we were, but we weren't.

But one thing came out of it. I realised I could write. I realised I could write lines that made people laugh. From then on I couldn't stop. For a while Peter wrote with me, but I believe he got a little bored because it all took so long and reject slips from radio and TV were depressing. After a while Peter and I moved to London to try our hand at writing in the City. It didn't work. Peter decided to go back to sea and earn some cash. I stayed in London and continued to write. I had some success by writing a pilot script

THE SCRIPT WRITERS (comedy). Peter McKay and me in serious mode. (Photo:- Scrivens & Son.)

for a puppet called JuJu, the Kinkerchu. It took me nearly two years to get my money.

My interest in things spiritual and my quest for inner knowledge never let up. By now I was beginning to write poetry – why, I never knew. I never had any real passion for verse, but suddenly it became very important and much that I wrote concerned the journey of the soul. It became so important to me that I brought together a small collection, titled it *Just Another Poet* and had it published in Herne Bay by Ridout & Son. I became a one man publicity machine. One thing I learnt early on about poetry is that everyone loves a poet, but not everyone wants to buy his work. So, armed with a stack of wafer thin volumes, I did the rounds of bookshops, begging them to take my book on a sale or return basis. Most shops agreed, thankfully. Then I sent copies to local newspapers, which gave me a little publicity.

I started writing comedy verse, one of which was used by The Barrow Poets, a performing group of poets and musicians who were very popular at that time, appearing on TV and radio. I received 25p every time they used it. The poem was called *The Highwayman*.

> The highwayman came riding
> Over the misty moor.
> He'd had his oats
> In John O'Groats,
> And was riding back for more.

That poem made me, together with an airing on Woman's Hour, about £25.

THE SCRIPT WRITERS. Peter Mckay portrays the pain he felt on having a typewriter on his back! (Photo:- Chris Goldthorp.)

Whilst in London I decided to visit the owner editor of the Occult Gazette, one Mrs Spearman-Cook. She held weekly meetings at her home just off Kensington High Street. I had heard a lot about her and as I was living in London I decided to pay her and her organisation a visit. I entered a rather large palatial Georgian terraced house, stacked with antiques and cushion high carpets. The smell of incense greeted me and I was asked to remove my shoes as a sign of reverence. I paid my entrance fee and was ushered into a beautiful furnished inner chapel. Classical music was being played on a very expensive stereo system. When all were assembled we were asked by a helper for silence. A very definite hush fell upon the congregation as if they knew exactly what to expect, which of course most of them did. I heard a slight commotion behind me and decided to sneak a look.

Being carried on a Sedan Chair by four men was the famous medium and spirit teacher Mrs Spearman-Cook. She was gently settled in front of the small altar where she stretched up her arms and gave an invocation. Then the four male escorts turned her round to face us, her congregation. I don't remember everything that was said or was spoken through her, only that it was very depressing and gloomy, distinctly racial, and decidedly weird. She claimed that leukaemic blood – she suffered from leukaemia – was the only true blood (I said she was weird). She also claimed that the Moon was not real but was an illusion and that when the first manned rocket tried to land there they would pass right through it. When, of course, our lads did land on the Moon and beamed back those fantastic pictures, Mrs Spearman-Cook then claimed that the spacemen had gone through a time barrier. They were, in fact, beaming back pictures of the past! (There is some speculation as to whether they really landed at all. I do think some of the 'still' photos are a bit iffy, and wonder how the astronauts survived the huge amount of radiation on the Moon.)

I visited her meeting house twice. I was also interested to hear that George Harrison and Alan Whicker had paid her a visit. What they had made of her I shall never know. After my second visit, she closed the meeting with her usual dramatic benediction and her four burly men carried her back up the aisle. But as they got halfway up I realised they had stopped. I heard a male voice say "Excuse me, young man". I looked up straight into the eyes of Mrs Spearman-Cook. She held my gaze for a few seconds, then without a word waved her bearers on. Why she stopped I don't know. Maybe she sensed my hostility. Suffice to say, I never returned. I had had a gutful of Mrs Spearman-Cook!

CHAPTER 5

*D*reams and astral travel have been the subject of much debate for thousands of years and not until Freud and Jung were they brought to the fore. Most psychiatrists and psychologists today would admit Freud's preoccupation with sexual symbolism, phallic and otherwise, is really only a part of what the dream state can teach us. I am by no means any sort of expert on dreams, but symbolism most certainly does play a part. If a picture can speak a thousand words then a symbol can speak a thousand pictures.

One experience concerning dream symbolism happened in 1975. I dreamt I was drinking in a pub where I was suddenly approached by a creature that was one-third dog, one-third woman and one-third man: in the dream state everything is possible without exception. The creature started to talk to me and I found I was in no way afraid of this person/creature. In fact, we shook hands. I remember its hand being rather warm and clammy. I was not offended by this. The creature then took me over to a piano in the pub and started to play it - and play very well. I noticed that the piano had a sign on the side of it which said "petrol-driven". Then I woke up.

A few weeks later, my sister Josie asked me whether I would come over and have a drink at Charlie Morris's new pub (I usually have a soft drink, as I can't stand the taste of alcohol though I quite like the effect). Charlie was the finest publican I had ever met. He used to run *The Cardinal's Cap* in Canterbury which was frequented by all the actors and staff of the Marlowe Theatre. Sadly, his wife, Phil, was taken ill and Charlie had to give up The Cardinal's Cap and was asked by the brewery to run another pub nearby for a while. He was the kindest, most generous of men. Josie was helping him out behind the bar. I was told where the pub was and thought nothing of it when I was informed that it was called *The Black Dog*.

I arrived, ordered a bitter lemon and sat on one of the stools at the bar, just chatting generally to Josie and Charlie. It was about 9.30pm and the pub closed at 10.30pm. I was aware that there were two girls and a man seated at the other end of the bar. Suddenly I felt a very clammy, sweaty hand in mine. I turned around and there, just a tiny bit pissed, was one of the two ladies. She was about 25-ish, not strikingly good-looking, but not unattractive. I realised that she obviously had to shave her face. A slight darkish haze was beginning to show itself beneath her make-up. She was upset and needed someone to unload on and I was always a soft touch when it comes to listening. It became apparent as the evening came to a close that she needed more than just someone to talk to. 10.30pm arrived, much to my relief.

The lady in question and her two friends 'phoned for a taxi, but with no luck. They had to walk quite a way to get home and, as I had to wait anyway for Josie to finish up, I offered to give them a lift. This I did and planted them safely outside their place of residence in Thannington. The couple got out, but the lady with whom I had spoken promptly got in again. I had to literally push her out of the car, with great good humour I should add. I arrived back at the pub, picked Josie up and took her home, had a quick coffee and was then off again home to Herne Bay. I switched on the car radio and twiddled the tuner. Nothing. All I could get was piano music. Wherever I tuned, no matter what wavelength, all I got was piano music. Then it struck me - the dream! - the creature! - a cross between a woman, a man and a dog. It was a woman that I met who had the male characteristic of having to shave. She also had clammy hands. The name of the pub was called The Black Dog and all I could get on the car radio was piano music. The sign on the piano in my dream read 'petrol-driven'. Surely it couldn't be plainer than that.

Telepathic communication between someone awake and someone asleep and dreaming was proven to me on a couple of occasions. Obviously, the bond between, say, a husband and wife, or in my case between mother and son, goes a long way to forging telepathic communication (remember the incident between our family and my brother's dog, Shadow?) My mother would often have bad sleep states where she would cry out for help. There is nothing quite so heart-rending as hearing someone cry out for help in their sleep, a sense of terrible helplessness and isolation. When this happened - and it happened many times - my mother's cries for help tended to wake me. At first I did nothing. Then I decided to mentally talk to her, reassuring her that I was there and that there was no need to fear. To my great surprise and relief she quietened down almost immediately. In fact, I would say that eight times out of 10 she responded favourably.

Then came the occasion that really got me going. Mother was crying out for help and I, right away, started my telepathic broadcast. "Help! help! help!" cried my mother. "It's alright mother," I said mentally, "I'm here. It's okay. Nothing can harm you now." "Paul what are you doing here?" came the immediate reply. "I heard you cry for help and thought I would come and see what I could do" I replied (again

My mother aged 15.

mentally). Mother replied (audibly remember). "Oh! Thank you" she said and then her voice faded into a mumble and there was silence. It took me a while to get back to sleep with the excitement of it all. With a slight variation this happened again on yet another occasion. My mother, sadly, remembered nothing in the morning. The self-erasing mechanism that affects dream consciousness was working as usual. How many times, I wondered, did mother cry out without waking me? What further conversations could we have had?

One event that I think is worth recording is to do with what I term as psychic domestic invasion. Most people at some time or another experience odd happenings in the home, such as familiar objects going missing for days, then turning up in strange places that nobody can explain; hearing footsteps on the stairs when all doors are closed and locked and everybody is assembled in the same room; perhaps hearing odd cracking sounds that changes in temperature cannot explain. These are fairly common and soon disappear. But why do they happen in the first place?

From 1961 to 1975 we all lived in Gilchrist Avenue, Herne Bay. We experienced a period when all of us seemed to be having bad sleep states. My mother was having a particularly bad time. On one occasion, I had to get out of bed (this was before I discovered mental communication with her during sleep) and go into her room. She was paralysed with fear and calling for help. I switched on the light. As the light went on, she said "Thank God! They were hanging a man above my bed and I couldn't move." After a few minutes, she went back to sleep and all was well. This was the climax to two weeks of bad sleep states and objects going missing. The main object that disappeared was our hairbrush. We have a sort of communal hairbrush in our house. Other things also vanished like tools or towels, but nothing serious.

Then came my dream. I had already heard my mother again calling for help (God knows what she gets up to in her sleep). After she had settled down, I drifted off to sleep. I found myself floating over a graveyard at night. Huge tombs predominated. The graveyard seemed to be situated between two church buildings. Next, I found myself inside a church listening, with some people I obviously knew, to a young priest reading a lesson from the Bible. Suddenly the small lights high up in the church roof began to fall and smash on to the church floor. A sense of fear and dread filled me. I knew something evil was afoot. People were leaving the church in panic. I gathered my friends about me, joined hands and began to pray. As I prayed, I woke up still praying. I was in a cold sweat.

The next day I decided enough was enough. This invasion of sinister psychic phenomena must end. I must block up this hole between the worlds that had been forced open. I believe there are many worlds between this one and the next and what we were experiencing, though rare, was not exactly uncommon. There are many types of consciousness, many of which are not human, but think and have their being just as we do. These mischievous souls (nature spirits and elementals) have as much right to their world of nature as we have to ours, but because of man's destruction of his/their/our natural environment; the tearing down of forests, the spreading of poisons on the ground and in the air; they are obviously hostile towards us and can you blame them?

I am not suggesting that in fact we were being invaded by nature spirits, for they are usually gentle, but that something unpleasant had forced an entry into our world for some reason I did not know. However, I decided to hold a small service of exorcism. This is simply done by taking a Bible in one's hand, sprinkling salt in each and every corner and asking that love, light and harmony fill the whole house, finishing with the sign of the cross (salt is a symbol of purity. It is not the salt itself, nor the presence of the Bible that works, but what they represent – even these trappings are merely a way of focusing and are not absolutely necessary). This I did. After this, my mother went upstairs to fetch something and there on her bed, as if to say "Okay, you win!", was our hairbrush. An hour before, my mother had hung curtains by standing on the same bed and couldn't possibly have missed it. It seems that 'they' had to have the last say. From then on everything was peaceful.

CHAPTER 6

*M*y next personal experience with exorcism concerned a particular house on Herne Bay seafront. In 1970, Martin Leadbeater, a friend of mine, was renting a first floor flat. He told me that he and his girlfriend were experiencing cold spots in various places and the uncanny feeling they were being watched. This made them and their flat somewhat uncomfortable. They asked me whether I would check it out and invited me to dinner. I accepted and went along the following week. Martin and his girlfriend, plus a few others, were gathered and we had a very nice vegetarian meal. Afterwards, Martin asked if I was ready and asked what they should all do. I arranged everybody in a circle (there was about six of us) and had the lights turned down. I opened with a small prayer and started to tune in. Almost immediately, I saw an old lady of around 75 with a bent back, wearing an old crossover overall which she wore with a 1930's-looking flowered dress. Her hair was grey and done up in a bun. As she drew close to me I could see that she was crying. I too began to cry because I was feeling what she was feeling.

She told me she didn't want to leave. It was her house and what were all these strangers doing in it? She impressed upon me that her house was being invaded without her permission. I understood that she had died many years ago, but, of course, time in the in-between world is much different from our rather slow conception of time here and 40 years would appear to her like so many months. She was upset and angry.

I pulled myself together and closed the meeting. I told Martin and those assembled that I would try to arrange for her to be gently taken to the 'other side', as the spiritualists call it. Later, I called upon the White Brotherhood to go to her. Three days later, I was seated meditating when Omid, my spiritual teacher at that time, came to me and told me that all was now well and that the lady had been gently taken to her final destination. With that, I got in the car and drove to the house on Herne Bay seafront. Martin opened the door. I asked him if the house was any quieter. He told me that the cold spots had disappeared and that the house was now warm and friendly. As far as I know it remained so.

A similar incident happened in a Welsh village near Aberystwyth. I had gone for a weekend with Bernie Shaw and his wife (at the time) Pip, to stay with Paddy Safka and her husband, Peter, who ran the Aberystwyth Art Centre. Paddy was a very beautiful singer, dancer, and actress, with legs that went on forever. She had a thalidomide son who only had hands where his arms should have been. (The last I heard, he was a drummer with a rock and roll band – honestly.) We arrived rather late after prowling over the dark mystic mountains of Wales. We were warmly greeted and given supper. Peter said that Bernie and Pip could have their room for the night and they would sleep on a double mattress downstairs in front of the fire. I was to sleep in their son's room. Pip and Bernie protested "Why should they give up their room for us?" "Oh, we don't mind," said Peter, "besides, it's haunted". That information went down like a lead balloon.

Apparently the room had recently been built on to this rather ancient Welsh cottage and ever since, they had experienced a strange presence and heaviness in the room. The room was also very cold. Although they slept there, Paddy and Peter were always aware of the strangeness of the room, so much so, that they had drawn a crucifix in chalk on the headboard of their bed. I suggested that I be allowed to go into the room to see what I could feel. They agreed. I walked into the centre of the room after closing the door and tuned in. I felt nothing evil there exactly, but there was a definite imbalance. The impression I got was the old cottage, through the years, had developed a kind of persona of its own, built up by the generations of people who had lived there, and suddenly a great hole had been made in its side and a new limb grafted on. It was through this wall that outside, other-worldly influences were seeping in, almost like a wound that would not heal and had gone septic, letting in some sort of infection. Simplistic it might sound, but that is the information I picked up.

I performed a small service of exorcism, praying in each corner, calling for light and harmony from the Infinite. I left the room and told Paddy and Peter what I had experienced and what I had tried to do. Peter went into the room for a few minutes. When he came out he proclaimed that the room was now "different". Bernie and Pip slept soundly in the room without any problem and came down to breakfast without a tale to tell, much to their relief. The room remained quiet for over a year. Then I received a letter from Paddy to tell me that it had started all over again. Soon after, they moved to another part of Wales.

I have done many a 'house clearance' over the years. That's not because I was in the second-hand business! No, as many of you know, people, for all sorts of reasons, become house-bound, or Earth-bound. They usually make their presence known by standing next to you and trying to communicate (the hairs on your head tend to stand up!). After a year or three, the entity (person) doesn't even bother trying to get through to you. Then, as time goes on (and 'time', as such, to them does not exist), by the art of practice born of frustration, they are able to move small objects. Anything to grab your attention. (This is nothing to do with poltergeist activity. That is quite a different phenomenon.) If that doesn't scare the hell out of you then turning the television on and off or flooding the house with light by turning every switch on, not just the usual lights but ALL of them, then it's guaranteed that will! Or if you're *really* stupid and not just psychically thick, pictures will start to fall off the wall and end up nowhere near where they were hung! Then either you call in a priest, or someone like me.

Of course, it *could* be psychological, ie. you have just *imagined* that there were cold-spots and someone was staring at you, or you just *imagined* the TV was switching itself on and off, or that you just *imagined* coming home and finding all the house lights on. Maybe you *imagined* everything! When a priest or psychic comes into the picture and does what they do to clear things up, then you're re-programmed to BELIEVE that they are a success and become psychologically well again... even though the pictures are still falling off walls, etc. Well, to enter a house of un-rest and put it right and then receive *proof* (in this case years later) that the information you initially received was correct is infinitely satisfying.

Many years after the Herne Bay and Wales incidents, I was called out with my friend Andy Thomas to a village in East Sussex called Fletching. Also with us was the dowser David Russell. The house belonged to friends of Andy and, as he was a musician, they often attended his gigs. They got talking and it transpired that their house was 'haunted': the TV was being switched on and off, doors were locking and unlocking, clothes were torn and a 'presence' was felt. The final straw came when what appeared to be a child's footprint appeared, deeply embossed in their rather thick carpet. Nothing would erase it.

I agreed to do what I could, but stated that there was no guarantee of success! We arrived and I settled myself down in an armchair and listened to what the friends of Andy had to say. Then I 'opened up' and allowed this presence to come closer. The presence (male) said that he and his small son had died in a fire in this house and could I help them? I said that they should look around until they saw a white door, or at least what appeared to be a point, or beam, of light. The man began to weep. As he left, he thanked me. He could obviously see the point of light. (Why, you may well ask, is not the death process automatic, as in 99.9% of people? I can only say that when people die in exceptional circumstances or when folk insist on holding on to Earth conditions, there is little they can do. They're probably *frightened* of the point of light or the white door, as well they might be; it is the great unknown, after all. They probably see it and ignore it until instructed otherwise). After I did what I did, the footprint in the carpet gradually started to fade and they had no more trouble!

The proof came years later when Andy met up with his friends again. Not only had the child's foot-print completely gone, but having spoken to locals in the years since, they had discovered that their house had been built on the site of an old abattoir (always a disrupter of psychic energies, for obvious reasons) and that before that a man and his little son HAD indeed died in a fire in a house which had stood previously on the same site... about 150 years ago. I now had proof that what the 'man' had told me was absolutely true, proof recorded in the village records.

My father and mother with me at Cheyney Hospital, Sevenoaks, Kent.

Back around the time of the Herne Bay and Wales events, I started voluntary work at Kent and Canterbury Hospital. Every Friday afternoon I went round Mount and McMaster Wards with the hospital menu to find out what the patients wanted to eat, a chore that was too time-consuming for the nurses. I enjoyed it and made a lot of friends among staff and patients. One day, whilst doing my rounds, I came across a gentleman who at first didn't say a word. I didn't take a lot of notice and rattled off the menu whilst he either nodded or shook his head. I then started to chat to him generally about his condition and his family life. He started to tell me about his family, then about his job. He was a professional gardener and clearly loved his work.

We chatted for a while, then I had to make my excuses as I had the rest of the ward to finish. He was obviously disappointed and asked me to come back and chat to him. I said I would try. "You don't understand," he said, "I haven't spoken a word since I have been in here. You are the first person I have talked to." I was surprised and very pleased that I had stimulated him into talking again. Sadly, I had yet another ward to do as the other volunteer was ill, so I never managed to get back to see him. That night I visited a small group of folk under the supervision and guidance of Gladys Franklin, a very talented psychic and teacher. During the meeting I was told clairvoyantly that my hands were bright green, the colour of fresh grass. I took little notice. A lot of freaky thing things are seen clairvoyantly.

That night, for some reason, I couldn't sleep. After a while I realised that there was someone in my room and that someone was the gardener from the hospital! He obviously still wanted to talk and had left his body in the hospital and tracked me down. I told him mentally that if he allowed me to sleep then we could, no doubt, talk until the proverbial cows

38

came home. I was just dropping off to sleep when I felt the bedclothes being dragged off me. I grabbed hold of them and pulled them back round me. My heart pounded as I sent the message "If you want to talk to me, please have the patience to let me get off to sleep." Eventually I did sleep. In the morning I remembered absolutely nothing, though in time it came back to me. Very often with psychic events they don't always have a conclusion. This was one of those. I never saw the gardening man again, but it is odd to think that this event was preceded by my having green fingers.

I experienced two significant incidents concerning the medium Gladys Franklin. Through mutual friends I was introduced to Gladys and her band of young followers and helpers whilst in my thirties. Gladys taught healing and instruction in the training of psychic and spirit faculties. I had heard a lot about her work and gifts and when asked to go to one of her meetings I accepted immediately. Gladys, like so many other mediums, is a very ordinary person to look at – white permed hair and glasses, and lots of cups of tea. Surrounded by her surprisingly young company of workers, she reminded me of everyone's favourite grandmother.

I enjoyed my first evening with her group and decided to go again. After a few months of gathering in a friend's house in Herne Bay, Gladys managed to rent Hoades Court, a large house in Babs Oak Hill, near Sturry. I attended meetings there for nearly a year and learnt much about myself and a little about my inner self. I did not agree with everything that Gladys taught or indeed what Chan, her Chinese guide, taught, but the atmosphere was always joyful and their healing work and service to so many spiritual groups and churches were second to none.

One day I woke up with great pain in the base of my spine. Nothing seemed to relieve it. The doctor gave me painkillers, but that was all. I phoned Gladys and asked if she would give me healing. She told me to come over right away. When I arrived Colin, Christine, Gary and Martin (Gladys's strong band of disciples) and, of course, Gladys were waiting for me. I was asked to lie down on their healing couch, which I believe had been specially charged with light. Colin stood at my feet and Christine at my head. Gladys, Gary and Martin sat facing me. The curtains were drawn and after a short opening prayer the healing began.

During the laying on of hands Gladys gave a running commentary of what was taking place. She described two doctors who had, apparently, inserted a tube into my stomach and were now draining it. (Of course, this operation was being performed on my etheric body and therefore I felt nothing). How this was supposed to heal my back I wasn't sure. After the session was over, within a few hours the pain subsided and by morning it had completely gone. But this was not the end of the story. What I had not told Gladys or her helpers was that for quite a few months I had been experiencing stomach pains. After the healing session, the pains completely disappeared. Now I understood why those spirit doctors took so much trouble over my stomach.

In another extraordinary incident, I foresaw events concerning Gladys and her company. I had just finished visiting an old gentleman that I knew, Will Coombes, who lived in a council run group of flats in the village of Hoath, about three miles from Hoades Court. I got into my car and was just about to start it when I saw Colin and the others pull up at a junction just in front of me. I waved, but they couldn't see me. Colin, who was driving the old black Ford Anglia, pulled round and passed me. Christine, sitting in the front, was leaning over the back seat talking to Gary and Martin. As they drove past I waved again – still they didn't see me. As I was on my way to see Gladys anyway I decided to follow them. I started the car, quickly backed round into the junction and hared off after them. I caught them up just on the brow of the hill coming out of Hoath. I could see Gary and Martin talking through the back window. Still they didn't see me.

They eventually pulled up at the T-junction. I pulled up behind them – still no response. Surprisingly, they turned right to Herne Bay. Hoades Court, where they all lived with Gladys, was the left turn. I imagined they had business elsewhere and so drove to Hoades Court. I arrived a few minutes later, walked the short distance to the front door and knocked. After a few seconds the door opened - and there stood Colin. I asked what on Earth he was doing there when I had just seen him driving to another town. He looked at me, shrugged his shoulders and told me that he had been there all afternoon. He asked me in and led me to the kitchen. There, seated, was Gladys, Gary and Martin. I gabbled out my story to them whilst still not believing my eyes.

They had been there all afternoon. There was no question of that. Christine, on the other hand, was in Gibraltar - and I knew that. I knew she was in Gibraltar, but seeing her there in the car with the others threw it completely out of my mind. I realised that what I had witnessed was my first experience (well, first *conscious* experience) of external clairvoyance and the message that accompanied it was simple. Almost too simple, in fact, for such an elaborate example of three-dimensional, full colour, stereophonic, clairvoyance. The message was that all Gladys's disciples would leave her within six months!

Sure enough, Christine was the first to leave. The rest followed in due course. The last I heard from Gladys for a while was a letter from her in Canada. She had started again with a new band of budding young mediums. Gladys Franklin, now in her 80's, is today back in England and carrying on with her work.

CHAPTER 7

I managed to get my first professional job as an actor with Hendrick Baker, the producer of *Toy Town* on BBC radio. The show had been running on and off in various mediums since 1928. Now, in 1971, an animated version was to be made for Thames Television. The animation was done by my Uncle Bob of Bura and Hardwick animations, already experienced with their work on *Trumpton* and *Camberwick Green*. I had just written a five-minute pilot script for my cousin, George Duboush, on a character called Professor Whodunit. The script was completed, but we had to find someone to do the voices of the Professor and the Genie. Messing around with voices was something I had always loved to do so I volunteered. We recorded the soundtrack with music written and played by Barry Cole on bass clarinet. Cousin George went to work on the animation.

When the film was completed we tried to sell it to various TV companies with no success. By chance, we happened to be running it at my Uncle Bob's studio in Hornsey, North London, when in walked Hendrick Baker. He hated the film, but loved the voices, especially the Germanic voice of the little Professor. He was looking for new voices for his forthcoming series, now renamed *Larry the Lamb*. He wanted me to audition for the main character voice of Dennis the Dachshund, the little German dog. I auditioned for the part and got it. I also did the voices in the series for the Doctor, Captain Higgins, Captain Brass, the

My first professional job: Larry the Lamb recordings. L.to R. Peter Hawkins, Patsy Blower, Wilfred Babbage, me.

highwayman and others.   Wilfred Babbage was the only surviving member of the original radio cast from way back in 1928 and played the Mayor and others.   Patsy Blower played Larry and Peter Hawkins, who started his voice-over career creating the voices for the famous *Flowerpot Men*, was Mr Growser, the Policeman and many, many others.   Peter taught me an awful lot about microphone technique.   From then on I started doing TV and radio voiceovers and film commentaries.

I was also writing more poetry.   *Mustn't Dent the Memory* sold well and *Behind the Joker* did even better.   I had now developed a style.   I was publishing privately and after the publication of *Under the Stairs* I started seriously to find a London publisher who would publish me in hardback and have some sort of distribution.

I was now 28 and suddenly I was plunged into the most horrific period of my life.   This was also my fourth seven year cycle.   I had been meditating for years using no particular technique.   I would just relax and go to a peaceful area inside my head.   I relaxed down and managed sometimes to tap unspeakable peace.   For some time I had been reading and hearing about the then *Beatles* guru Maharashi Mahash Yogi and his method of transcendental meditation, known throughout the world as TM.   I decided to give it a try.   After my initiation I was given a mantra (a word) with which to meditate on.   The results were quite wonderful.   The technique was certainly more powerful than my own self-taught method though the results in raised consciousness were similar.   TM got you there faster.

I was now meditating for 20 minutes twice a day.   I began to experience the most profound union with the Infinite.   It was as if I had become almost omnipresent.   I was part of all things and all things were a part of me.   The teaching had become a reality, yet I knew that I had only merely scratched the surface of my godself, making but a small dent.

After meditating in my car, parked in a wood, I would go home radiating with joy.   It was like being plugged into the Universe.   This profound mystical experience had happened perhaps, in its higher state, only three times in my life so far.   After the first time one cannot believe that something so beautiful could happen to a human being.   So much so that after a while one believes it was only a dream.   Then it is a privilege to have it happen again, which reinforces one's belief that it was no dream, but the greatest reality that one can experience, that this world is illusion, a lesser reality.   It was like listening to the most wonderful music one could imagine without hearing a sound.

But after the experience of ecstasy came nine months of the most profound horror that I could imagine.   It started with a slight faint feeling of fear just after meditating. At first I just shrugged it off, but then it became worse. So bad was it that I was reduced to a shrivelling crying wreck petrified of something that I could not see. I was surrounded by fear. I became afraid of being afraid! When I first experienced this terrible mental turmoil and pressure the thought came to me that if I had a gun I would put a bullet in my head. Anything would be better than this. I rejected the thought as soon as it was presented, but it emphasised my desperation and pain.

Physical pain I could endure. I was fairly used to it with my various ins and outs of hospital, but with this type of surreal mental torment I would have preferred to have my arms and legs torn off. This, at least, I could understand. The doctor thought I was experimenting with drugs. He never actually said so, but I knew what he was thinking and I couldn't blame him. After all, if a patient came to him and told him he was surrounded by fear, that he had freaked at the sight of a common household brick (I still don't know why), that he felt as though his head and mind were full of holes and that he was sensitive to every thought and emotion that appeared to pour through these holes (which appeared in my psychic self) - well, what would you think? He couldn't help me. I never knew when I would be attacked. I thought I was going insane.

I remember one occasion I was sitting in the kitchen when a rushing and a roaring sound started in my ears. My whole body was taut as a bowstring. I felt as though there was a hole in the middle of the floor and I was being sucked inextricably into it. If I allowed myself to go, my brain would snap and I would be insane. I was banging my head on the table, anything to make it go away. Yet all the while, throughout all the torment of the mind-splitting pain, I knew that I was never alone.

"My God. My God. Why hast thou forsaken me? Have I not followed thy way? Have I not loved thee?"

Always, but only just perceptibly, I was aware of something (a 'watcher') that told me that I would come out of it, that all this was necessary, that I had the strength to conquer and come to terms with it and, above all, understand it.

I got in touch with my initiator into TM. I was told that I would not suffer more than I could bear. Well, that was great news! Here was I on the brink of going crazy and all I was told was that I would not suffer more than I could bear. I understood that there was a certain amount of stress that would be thrown up by my nervous system, but this was beyond anything that I had ever experienced. It would appear that trying TM, to my system, was like a hot knife going through butter. I had already loosened up much of my life's stress with my own form of meditation, but now it was coming away in huge wads and I was suffering horribly. My family were powerless to help me. They could only support me with their love and this they did admirably.

In desperation, I went to see Eileen Newport, the leader of the developing circle I had joined a few years earlier. Perhaps she could help me, tell me something. She had told me that I had met the 'Dweller on the Threshold'. She gave me no more information than that. At first I thought it was some kind of evil being who was plundering my senses; that I was in mortal combat with an invisible enemy. Many, many years later I came to understand who that enemy was, who the dweller on the threshold was, who was dealing me such mighty blows. It was myself. I was in conflict with my own ego. I was in the process of killing off a part of myself that I no longer needed.

I happened upon a book called *The Shining Brother*. It was about a communication from St Francis of Assisi (known to some as the 'ascended master' Koot Hoomi). I came across the following quote: *"The experience met with at this period will consist of events which will force him or her to face themselves and to bring to their consciousness every secret and open fault. Events which will force them to gaze into the eyes of the self he has created which contains the essence of the desires, ambitions, passions, and aspirations of their personality. It is the Dweller on the Threshold that each must meet, recognise as their own creation and conquer."*

I had realised for some time that I was undergoing a change. I no longer wanted to perform at a drop of a hat, do five minutes when the

fridge light went on. If I went to a pub I was always expected to be the joker, to tell gags and to make everybody laugh. I enjoyed laughter. Laughter is a wonderful thing, but I needed more time to myself. There was a serious side to my nature, but people didn't want that. They wanted the old Paul, a song, a dance, a poem and a quick prophecy! Well, I had had enough. I would only perform when I wanted to and usually only professionally.

From the quote from St Francis of Assisi I wrote the following summary: *"From the moment we are born we at once become moulded by our parents and those around us. Later on we either reject or accept the prompting of the all-powerful ego to create of*

Entertaining some old folks with naughty poetry.

ourselves what we think others want us to be even though it may well go against the grain. For a time we indulge the ego, we let it run free, but inside the suffering grows, the growing grows until the bubble bursts with the pressure of being somebody that you don't like. That person you don't like is the monster that still looms largest in your consciousness. It is most powerful, created with the force of the highest passions and desires and takes so much spiritual strength that one becomes almost stifled to a point that one could almost take one's life to be free of this terrible conflict between the monster and the real self. The monster, although you hate your creation and, because it is still very close to you, hate yourself, is so very hard to let go and kill off. Ego will still not let you let go of it. People will say you have changed and for some folks, those who liked your extravagant and over-the-top ways, the old monster will still rear its head in order to please them. But in time a kind of order takes place. One must learn to love the real self, the new real self. Ego is a necessary commodity in the human soul, but the soul, the real you, must be in control of ego and not the other way round."

I would not wish this kind of suffering on my worst enemy and it took me four years to be able to say "I am glad I went through that". I learnt so much about myself. Myself, for me and my relationships to other people.

My sister Mellie (who also practised TM) suffered in much the same way and for a long time found it difficult to even go to a cinema or theatre unless she was near the exit in case she was attacked. At least I could tell her she was not alone, that her suffering was not so isolated as she thought and this gave her comfort. We both became stronger people as a result.

In order to throw off the remnants of this period I wrote a comedy, the complete reverse of what I felt. It did the trick. 'Charlie' (my pet name for the monster) never returned.

The ego is the emotional self, containing greed, envy, jealousy, pride, vanity and all those emotions that cause us pain and odd behaviour; always competing with the next man; always calling for attention; always screaming to be heard like a spoilt child. Most of us still retain the out-of-control emotions that we experience when children. As adults we are supposed to have them under control, but as adults we become clever at concealing them, not understanding, but covering them up as though they don't exist. That, in my view, is when the trouble starts.

I also believe that we carry over passions and desires with us from previous lives that have not been tamed. That is why brothers and sisters of the same parents who have all been raised exactly the same can be so diversely different.

CHAPTER 8

And so to the question of reincarnation. One of the greatest experiences of my life happened one Sunday morning a few years ago. Prior to this experience, I had been having recurring dreams of finding myself dressed as a monk sitting on the stone steps of a ruined church. Around me lay fallen masonry covered in moss and green mould. There were great holes in the roof and rain was pouring in. Autumn leaves were blowing down the steps and I was weeping bitterly. I would wake up weeping.

One Sunday morning I was woken by the phone ringing by my bed. It was Peter McKay, my very old friend. With his wife Linda he was running a pub called *The Endeavour* in the small village of Wooton, near Folkestone. Peter sounded terrible. "Peter what's the problem?" I asked, heavy with sleep. "It's Linda. She's left me, taken Nathan (their son) and gone". He sounded like he was drowning. I told him to stay where he was and that I would be over immediately. I got dressed as quickly as I could, got in the car and was off. Wooton from Herne Bay was about three quarters of an hour away. I had to go through the picturesque and beautiful village of Patrixbourne, a joy at any time of the year, but this time it was different.

You must remember that all I was concerned about was getting to Peter as quickly as I could. My mind was on nothing else. But as I entered Patrixbourne I began to feel distinctly strange. As I travelled through (and one cannot drive fast through Patrixbourne) I was suddenly aware of the rather old walls along the side of the road, the tops of which were all covered in moss. Further on, I could see where more moss and green mould (Patrixbourne is very near running water) had formed on the tiles over windows. By now I was feeling very odd as if something extraordinary were about to take place.

As I took the first right hand bend I caught a glimpse of the church. That was it! The sight of the church was like a trigger in my head. It was as if I were watching a video of myself dressed as a priest preaching to a congregation in a church, *my church*. The difference was that not only was I viewing this scene, but I was also reliving it. Suddenly the doors of the church burst open and soldiers poured in and started to rush toward me. I was aware that I was teaching to my congregation that which I had always taught, but because of some ecclesiastical political law that had been passed I was now considered a heretic. The soldiers dragged me out of the church and I was tortured (I believe with boiling water, though I was not sure of this) and thrown into a cell. There were bars on the window and straw in one corner.

Somehow, I don't know how, I escaped and made my way to a

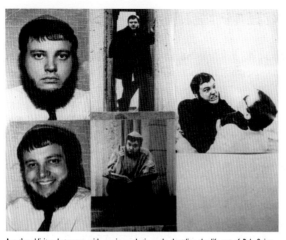

Agent's publicity photos: one with me in psychotic mode throttling the life out of Bob Onion.

monastery where I stayed for seven years (seven again). But then the urge to return to my church became too strong. I had to return. It was my church, they were my people and I loved them. So, dressed as a monk, I started to walk. I walked and walked until I finally arrived at my church. The sight that greeted me shook me to the soul. They had torn it down. They had destroyed my church. It was now but a ruin. I stumbled inside, what was left of it, and saw the fallen masonry and devastation. I sat on the stone altar steps. The leaves of autumn blew around me. Rain came through the roof and I wept. So there I was, with one foot in the distant past and one foot in the twentieth century, driving a car with tears streaming down my face.

All that I witnessed probably took no more than a minute at most yet it took me the rest of the journey (some 20 minutes) to compose myself. Here was one of the most profound happenings I had ever experienced and yet I now had to go and comfort a dear friend whose wife had just left him. I could not tell Peter about it, not yet at any rate, but with a good deal of help I managed to pull myself together and help in some small way to get Peter through this awful time.

What I believe took place is very simple. I had just been woken from a rather deep sleep state and rather suddenly too. Although I was awake, part of my consciousness was still connected to my unconscious self, the self that retains all memory of past lives. The channel was still partially open. All it needed to set this particular mental video memory into replay was the right trigger. That trigger was the decaying walls of Patrixbourne and finally the view of the church itself. Although I have told this tale a hundred times I am still moved by it.

Many years later a girlfriend of mine – a student at the Canterbury School of Art, film and video section, asked me to re-enact the whole thing. The 'steps' scene where I had to weep profusely, was shot in Canterbury in the ruins of St Augustines with my girlfriend chucking leaves at me. The church scene was shot in the actual church in the village of Patrixbourne where I had to read a sermon denouncing Henry the Eighth and swearing my allegiance to the Pope. By the way, through regression I now know who let me out of jail - it was a soldier who was also a fan of the Pope!

CHAPTER 9

A book of poems called *Breaking Through* came my way. It was written by a man called Derek Neville. I was so taken with these beautiful, down to earth, spiritual poems that I wrote to him via his publisher. Very soon I received a reply. He lived at Itteringham Mill in the village of Itteringham in Norfolk. He thanked me for my letter and comments and was perceptive enough to realise that I wanted him to read something of mine. He asked very politely, with reserve, to send him something of my own work. I sent him a copy of *Behind the Joker*, my latest collection to date.

Not only was Derek a writer and publisher, he also sold books. He asked if he might be able to sell some of my work at Itteringham Mill which turned out to be a wonderful vegetarian guest house open to the public. Beautiful and exciting salad lunches and teas were served on the lawns overlooking the river on which the mill stood. Fish in their hundreds would rise to the surface to be fed. Ducks and geese were everywhere. The mill was blessed with harmony and joy. People came from all over England to stay with Derek and his wife Mary.

Derek was the first true mystic I had ever met in the flesh. Not only did he like my work, but he invited me to stay for a couple of days, even sending me £10 to cover my petrol. I returned the £10, which I think upset him. It upset him in that he thought he had upset *me* by sending money. On reflection, I should have accepted such a generous offer in the spirit in which it was given. But we became good friends. He praised my work and told me that he did not give praise lightly. This was of great moment to me. Derek was the author of many, many books on the spirit including *The Ceaseless Beauty, The Garden of Silence, The Temple of the Soul, Honky* (the very moving story of a grey lagg goose who was found badly injured at Itteringham Mill) and, in 1977, the republication (after his death) of *Bright Morrow*, his first full length novel forged in the light of the spirit. I was asked to write the foreword for this latest edition. I felt very privileged to do so.

As a young man Derek set out to live the life of a tramp, living with down-and-outs, and sharing their life. He sold pen and ink poems for sixpence each, door to door. He always maintained that this was perhaps the richest period of his life and one of the happiest. He experienced the joy of the infinite in the lowest of conditions and through this realised the absurdity of material things.

Derek was the only man I had met who knew oneness in its almost perfect, earthly sense. He knew what it was to become a blade of grass;

indeed to become the meadow itself; to be the song in the throat of a bird as it tumbled out to express itself in the realms of nature; to know a tree as a personal friend. In his small magazine *Inspiration*, that had readers from all over the world, he said *"I believe in a realm of inspiration that exists within our own lives, a great reservoir of creative power whence springs all the truth and beauty we may ever know."*

Derek did not live his life in a state of prayer with hands clasped. His altar of reverence lay in the fields, in the hills, in the woods, and what he saw was a reflection of himself, of all of us – a bright droplet of the eternal, never changing, yet always changing. His great love affair with the kingdoms of nature rang sure and clear and we all heard it. He made sure of that, through his life and work. Yet I have to say, having written the above, I am immediately given the picture (as related by Jenny Porcus, a friend of us both) of Derek scraping burnt scrambled eggs out of an equally burnt saucepan after a hectic day at the mill. The everyday things never cease.

Derek's lovely wife, Mary, who had suffered from a heart complaint died suddenly. Some months later, after giving up Itteringham Mill, Derek too received his call. As a result I wrote the following poem:

THE PASSING OF DEREK NEVILLE
(Poet, Mystic, and Friend)

I woke and came downstairs
To the clatter and squawk
Of a bird fighting a windowpane
To get out! He had earned his freedom
I let him out!

On the mat
A letter from Derek
(his last words to me on paper)
And a cheque for six of my books.
The letter did not hint of a journey,
Not even the finest of brains
Could have read between HIS lines,
Read anything that wasn't there.

Side by side on the mat, along
With the newspaper and a bill,
Was a letter from a close friend
Of Derek and myself informing me
That he had passed!

What can I say?
What can I do?
Derek has said it all,
Has he not?
If anyone 'knew', Derek did.
How many times did he glimpse
The Eternal,
How many times did he
Bring it back to us?
His body will make
His beloved Earth
That much richer,
But his spirit will surpass
And enrich all things,
Here and beyond this Earth.

Goodbye my friend,
I shall listen
For your voice in the wind
When nature demands
That I write of her.
Speak softly
And I shall hear you roar,
Speak clearly
For those who missed out
On what you had to say.

Someone opened a window
And a bird flew to freedom!

Derek was to have published my then latest collection of poems *The Coming of the Giants*, but this was not to be. After his death, I was invited to his funeral along with many other of his close friends, among them Gwen Hart, Mary Wooler and Jenny Porcus. I intended to read the above poem at the funeral, but that also was not to be.

I started out in the car at about 8.30 in the morning on a very hot, beautiful, summer's day. My mother decided to come along too, together with my sister Josie. I drove to Canterbury via the old Thornden Wood road in order to pick Josie up. I came to a set of traffic lights on red – five minutes passed, then 10. Obviously something was wrong. I took a chance and drove over the red light, arriving some 15 minutes late to pick up Josie, then off we went. We arrived at the Blackwall Tunnel, found the correct road for Norwich and set off. After about an hour, I realised we were going in the wrong direction even though previous road signs had pointed to the contrary.

I turned around and headed back, picked up the signs again and made another attempt at Norfolk. Then the oil warning light came up on the dashboard. I pulled into a garage and filled up with oil, feeling very puzzled as I had checked the oil before setting out. Off we set again. More signs appeared to be totally wrong or pointing in the wrong direction. This meant more back tracking. Then the oil light came up again and again I had to fill up with oil. In all I filled up three times. I was obviously losing it somewhere. By now, time was running short. The funeral was only an hour away and we weren't even in Norwich. By the time we got to Norwich there was only half an hour to spare and the village of Itteringham lay outside of the town. This being only my second visit, I was still not familiar with the road and my map and written instructions were proving pretty hopeless.

In desperation, I asked a lady attending flowers in her front garden the way to Itteringham. "Just a minute, I will phone and find out for you," she said and disappeared inside her house. Five minutes passed, then 10, then 15. I was about to pull away when she reappeared clutching directions and apologising for her delay. I thanked her and set off again for Itteringham knowing in my heart that we would now never make it in time. When we finally arrived the service was over and the men were filling the grave. Together, with mother and Josie, I paid my last respects.

We were tired, hot and thirsty and I wanted very much to show Mother and Josie Itteringham Mill. So off we went for tea and sandwiches. The mill, of course, was not the same without Derek, but it was still beautiful. We sat inside at a table away from the other customers. Suddenly I felt someone tap me on the shoulder. I turned expecting to see an old friend of Derek's, but there was no-one there. Then I realised that Derek had made himself known for the last time. I silently acknowledged him.

After tea and a nostalgic look around the mill, I asked someone where I might find a garage who would look at my VW Beetle. A small country garage was pointed out and off we set. The man at the garage looked underneath my car and informed me that the rockerbox head had come off and that was why I was losing so much oil. But what was I to do? Where could a small country garage get hold of a VW spare rockerbox cover and fit it in the space of two hours? To my amazement, the mechanic said that he knew of two VW Beetle engines in a back garden only half an hour's drive away. One of them must have its rockerbox complete. I said that I was desperate and would be grateful if he could retrieve one for me. So off he sped on his motorbike, leaving us to enjoy the last of the day's sunshine. Within an hour he was back clutching a rust-covered rockerbox cover. He fitted it in 15 minutes, filled up with oil and charged me a very nominal sum for all his trouble. "The odd thing was," said the mechanic, "that the rockerbox came off in the first place. The replacement went on very tightly. How the other one came loose I shall never know." Well, if he didn't know I certainly didn't. All I did know was that for some strange reason I was not supposed to attend that funeral. I never knew exactly why.

Mary Wooler, who lived with Derek and Mary at the mill for many, many years, suggested that my poem would not have been acceptable to some of Derek's older friends and perhaps this was the reason. On re-reading my poem for him, I found this difficult to accept.

[Much of Derek's work is still available and can be purchased by writing to: Pene Sydenham, Beagle Burrow, Church Street, New Buckenham, Norfolk, NR16 2BA.]

Another man I befriended late in his life, but at the opposite end of the spectrum, left an impression on me. It was 1973, and my friend Peter McKay and his then wife Linda were managing a pub in the Dover area. I was invited over for the afternoon and was sitting in a sort of garden area when I *spotted* him. I say spotted him, but it was more to the point that I HEARD him before I spotted him. It was a kind of staccato with the edges rounded, a machine-gun sort of voice and he SHOUTED when he got excited, which was more often than not. He was wearing a bright pink track-suit and looked, facially, like a bank manager with bright, sparkling, energetic, and above all, intelligent eyes. He looked as though he was in his late 50's and his new wife (whose name I'm ashamed to say I've forgotten) appeared to be in her late 40's. I was correct with her age, but way off the mark regarding his! He was over 70.

Peter introduced me to him. It was like being verbally plugged-in to Battersea Power Station. Such was the power of this man's personality that I was completely taken off guard. He drowned me. Not in some vicious way, but in a kindly, open way. This was Victor Carasov. A small-time hotel thief who had spent over 50 years of his life in jail. 50 years of brutality and deprivation, 50 years of being considered mad at one time and just eccentric the other, 50 years of institutionalized banality. A few months on the outside and then IN again. From a converted war-ship where he was sent for stealing a bicycle when aged 11 to get away from a step-mother who smothered him in religion and God, to jail after jail after jail after jail. Do you pity him or despise him? Victor takes no pity. Despise him? You can't despise a man like Victor Carasov. Impossible, absolutely impossible.

Peter asked him if he could buy a copy of his book *Two Gentlemen to See You, Sir (the story of a villain)*. Peter gave him the money for the book. Victor disappeared for three hours. Everyone thought the worse. Everybody thought that he'd gone off with the money; even me! But he had a new wife and what do you do with a new wife on your honeymoon? He came back in the early evening with the book duly signed: 'To Peter and Linda. With the money I shall buy some food! VICTOR CARASOV.'

One thing Victor Carasov and I had in common.

He went slightly off-the-rails towards the end. His wife had left him and he was doing a short spell inside. He'd robbed a small hotel. Old habits die hard. I wrote to him there and he wrote back. He was very depressed. When he came out, he was in his mid-70's and after years of rejecting God within him, he embraced Catholicism. He came to see me in Herne Bay and I learned a bit more about him. For instance, he played the clarinet. I too played the clarinet! But he was lonely too, very lonely. He didn't admit to it. But I knew. Laughing and shouting in my front room was too much for my mother; she escaped to the kitchen. He was TOO much for her.

When at last I said goodnight, I didn't think that I would hear from him again. I was wrong. He rang me and wanted to come over. I shielded the mouthpiece of the phone and said quietly: "It's Victor, he wants to come over!" One look from my mother and that was it, finito. I tried to explain to him about the problem, making up any excuse that I could. It was with a heavy heart that I put down the phone. I felt so guilty. If I'd been on my own he would have been welcome, but...

About a year later, I received a letter from two ladies who owned a café. Victor used to come in for his meals. I guess he must have told them about me or how could they have known where to write? They said Victor was ill. Then I got a letter from a priest saying that Victor had died and would I like to write something in the church magazine?

When Victor was buried, it was on Good Friday. The clouds gathered in the afternoon and there was thunder, lightning and rain. At 3 o'clock precisely, the sun came out, a shaft of light lit up the church and hit Victor's coffin, which shone brilliantly. The thief on his cross was accepted into paradise by his Lord.

I can't exactly remember what I wrote in the parish magazine, but it ended with: "Death where is thy sting, grave where is Victor?" Arrogantly, I know the answer to that particular question.

CHAPTER 10

*I*n December 1979, my fifth seven-year cycle, we opened *Manna*, a whole and health food store in Herne Bay, with my old writing partner, Peter McKay. Just three short days after, I lost the strength in my arms. It was like having polio all over again. My left arm, which had always been Herculean in strength, mainly because I used it to pull myself upstairs, was now weaker than my right arm which until then I had always called my weak arm. There was no pain involved, only the sudden knowledge that from now on my life would change. My left arm was so weak I couldn't lift it above my head.

My balance had always been extremely bad, but if on the rare occasions I fell over or at least tripped, my arms would shoot out and clutch hold of anything in sight, human or otherwise, in order to prevent me from falling. This of course no longer happened. If I fell now it was like a tree being chopped down. There was nothing to stop it. For the first three weeks I was very depressed and also angry, not so much because of what had happened to me, but because people were having to do things for me that before I would never have dreamt of asking. Picking things up off the floor was a typical example. Then I began to realise that there was nothing I could do about this. I had to accept it.

Besides, why should I deprive people of helping me? Why should I deprive them of the gift of giving? Letting go and accepting something for what it is, is possibly the hardest lesson to learn. The pain of resistance is far harder than the objects of resistance - in my case my arms. When I let go to the situation and accepted it then my life gradually got on the road again. No doctor at this point had any idea what had happened and I just *had* to get on with it. Although I accepted the situation, I suddenly

realised for the first time in my life what it felt like to be a cripple. I had never thought of myself as a cripple. I had a disability, yes, but I never really gave it much thought. I had always said that having polio at the age of seven was far easier than having it at 18 because at 18 one had usually started some sort of career and polio would certainly put an end to that, whatever it was. That surely would have been a real test of courage – but not when you were seven.

But this seven year cycle also

Peter and I go into the wholefood trade. We ran a stall to advertise the opening of our shop.

brought its good side. Although the use of my arms was now restricted, I started to study nutrition and vitamin therapy, together with the use of herbs, to see whether I could help myself. Actually, nothing I learned helped my arms in any way, but the knowledge gained was invaluable in the new business venture. After three years, our little shop sometimes resembled a doctor's waiting room. We were able to help many folk using simple remedies, where doctors were failing. By a simple change of diet or the taking of certain vitamins and herbal teas, people's lives were subtly changed for the better. So, out of something bad came something good.

I believe that 50% of the healing process is the relationship between doctor and patient. Sadly, today doctors have so little time to form such a relationship. In our little shop we *made* time... and a lot of friends!

CHAPTER 11

*D*espite my weakened condition, I was still managing to do recording work plus co-presenting *Sounds, Words and Movement* for Radio 4. About this time, I was approached in the shop by a man with intense blue eyes, who my sister Josie had sent to see me in the hope that he might help with my arms. This man turned out to be one Tony Vernon-Vaughn, a man who was in the process, so he told me, of completing his training as a hypnotherapist. He suggested that my arm problem could be psychosomatic. I said that all things were possible and asked him whether he thought he could help. He said he was not sure, but if I were willing he would give it a try. There was no money involved. I would pay him only if he succeeded. This seemed very fair and I certainly had nothing to lose.

Tony was renting a room in William Street, Herne Bay, and was given the use of a front room for clients, me being the first. My first session with Tony was really a getting-to-know-you meeting, a general talk, establishing what made me tick. Being very interested in the workings of the mind I answered every question with complete honesty, throwing in odd idiosyncrasies about myself that even I thought strange. On the second occasion, Tony put me into what he termed a 'light hypnotic state' merely by having me close my eyes and gently talking to me, taking me through stages of relaxation. Whether he actually put me under I was never really sure, but at this stage I really wasn't bothered. I would visit Tony about twice a week and after the second week he attempted to get my left arm to rise. The method used was not unusual with what I understood about hypnotherapy. Tony would use the imagination to create a journey:

"You are going *down* a river in a boat, you stop and get out on to the river bank which runs *down* to a house. At the house, you walk in the front door. Just inside the door is a lift. You get in the lift which takes you *down* to the basement. When you arrive at the basement you walk *down* some stairs and come out into a beautiful secret garden..." As you can see, the journey was designed to take you *down* to the unconscious mind. Whilst in the 'garden', Tony would then talk to my left arm, trying to coax me to raise it. He never managed to do so, but nobody could say he didn't try. On one occasion, I have to admit that I did lose consciousness, but as I was lying down in front of the fire with the lights off, listening to Tony talking me down, I could well have just dropped off to sleep. I came to with Tony calling my name.

During the first three months we covered many subjects together. Tony was no intellectual, indeed neither was I. He was friendly enough and I grew to like him and look forward to my visits, but I found nothing extraordinary about him, only his desire to help me, which was kindness itself.

In our time together we touched on psychic and spiritual matters. Tony told me once that he had seen a cross made of clouds appear in a perfectly blue sky. After a few minutes the cross appeared to be sucked away. He also told me of an empty gravy boat that had shattered in front of him and couldn't be fitted together again. I found these experiences interesting, but no more than that. (He also told me that he had no family). It seems that any job he undertook, he somehow managed to be better than anyone else. Even as an ice-cream salesman he was offered the job of manager after only a few weeks, as he was capable of selling ice-cream so well and in such vast quantity. He was also, he claimed, the best student of hypnotherapy that Blythe College had produced to date. I had no reason to doubt any of this – why on Earth should he lie to me?

I introduced a very close girlfriend of mine to Tony in order that he might help her to relax (she had just gone through a minor breakdown). This he attempted to do. I am not sure he succeeded, but I shall return to this episode later.

One evening we were sitting together, drinking tea and chatting generally, when I mentioned the subject of shape-power (*see Chapter 12*), or, to be more precise, pyramid power. I also broached the subject of spiritual healing. Tony was obviously very interested in both subjects and I discussed them with him at some length. By now our sessions together were more informal chats. I think we both knew that he couldn't help my condition.

One evening we were sitting chatting together when I was suddenly aware that we were not alone. "There is someone else here," I said. "Yes, I know," answered Tony, "who is it?" I told him that I knew it sounded crazy, but I thought it was Carl Jung, the famous psychiatrist and contemporary of Freud. I was also aware that Jung (if it was Jung) wished to speak through Tony. I told Tony this. Tony said that he felt odd, but was quite happy for this to happen. I sent up a silent prayer that all would be well. Within a very short time Tony's expression changed. He appeared to be over-shadowed.

I asked who it was and could they please speak to me. Tony spoke in a slight German accent: "My name is Carl Jung." I asked where he was born. There was a pause, then he answered "From my mother's womb." I laughed, pleased that we had a sense of humour here. I persisted: "Where were you born?" He evaded the question and mumbled something about healing. Then he was gone. Tony's eyes were closed and it took him a while to come to. He was not aware (or so he said) of what had taken place, but was very interested and excited that he had been chosen as a mouth-piece for Jung. I told him I was not convinced it was Jung because he seemed somewhat evasive, but Tony seemed convinced that it was. I asked him if he wished to continue with this, to which he replied that he most certainly did.

Over the next two sessions Jung came through. He spoke of a new type of healing that would be used through Tony. In what form this was to take place was never clear. At this stage I was almost convinced that something wonderful was about to happen. At one point, I saw clairvoyantly a whole line of healers down through the ages, including Greeks and Romans, standing behind Tony with plenty of Light. This pleased me very much but then a new personality began to emerge. This was one of those stock-in-trade Chinese wise men. He called himself Lao-se-po. He was full of proverbs and old Chinese courtesy. He claimed also to be associated with Jung and the healing fraternity. Tony was now beginning to say rather outrageous things like: "Man can now make a nuclear bomb powerful enough to blow up the sun"; also that he (Tony) had once worked as a carpenter and wasn't Jesus a carpenter? I didn't like the sound of this. He seemed to be changing, getting above himself, before anything of real value had taken place.

A few weeks later yet another personality came through. This entity was called Keth(da)naynay. He claimed to be an Aztec priest and was here to operate on Tony so that the particular type of healing that was to come would manifest itself more directly.

During one session with Tony, Keth(da)naynay, using Tony's body, began to stomp about the room chanting. This went on for about half an hour, then Tony appeared to revert to himself for a while and insisted on lying on the floor. "They wish to operate on me" he said. I was in no position to intervene. Tony lay on the floor. Personalities came and went. I decided to tune in clairvoyantly; I saw a man dressed in black robes very much like a Greek Orthodox priest, bending over Tony and applying small sharp wooden needles to his body, a little like acupuncture. I also saw what appeared to be a glass dome lowered over his head. Why, I didn't know. Tony lay like this for over an hour. At one stage he turned over saying he could feel a weight on his chest. After another half an hour he started to shake with cold. He opened his eyes. I helped him up as best I could and he sat by the fire to warm up. When he was fully recovered, I left.

The next day I received a call from a lady to say that Tony was staying with her and her daughter and that he appeared to be talking like a Chinaman all the time. I said I would be right over. When I arrived at the house in Station Road, Tony opened the door to me, bowed very low and in the voice of Lao-se-po bade me enter. Lao-se-po told me that the Holy Ghost and Tony was the incarnation of Jesus. To my mind it would appear that Tony had flipped. His ego had taken over. I listened to the Chinaman entity and realised that there was no real intelligence here. I asked what had happened to Jung. I was told that his work had finished. I left saying I would return the next day.

I have to say that I never sensed any real evil here. It was somewhat disturbing, but not evil. However, I had my doubts about this. I contacted a musician friend of mine, Maurice Memmot, who a few years ago was associated with a so-called spiritual group in Thanet. 'So-called' because they strove for spiritual knowledge but something went wrong. One evening Maurice attended one of these meetings (I don't believe he was a full member, more an interested party) and observed a man dressed all in black. He looked more like a business man. Something happened that night, for all those associated closely with that group began to die mysteriously over a period of time. Maurice was outside the group and sensed that all was not well with this man in black. Maurice was now concerned with the man in black that I saw. Could it be the same man now associated with Tony? I suggested that Maurice accompany me to see Tony. This he readily agreed to.

We arrived the next day as arranged. Tony was still doing his Chinaman routine. After talking to him for a while it was obvious that Tony was being manipulated by a low elemental intelligence and Maurice agreed with me (certainly at this stage) that there was no real evil here but certainly cause for concern.

Tony stayed with the Chinaman personality for nearly a week. Then I received the next phone call. "He thinks he is Jesus," said the lady of the house. "I will be right over," I said. Tony was now talking like Tony although he occasionally lapsed into a stronger voice, at one stage stating that he and I got drunk together in a village over 4000 years ago.

I said my super-memory was not that active and that I didn't remember. Maybe I had a 4000 year old hangover! Tony told me to my face that he was Jesus returned. This phenomena is called the 'Jesus Syndrome' in the world of hypnotism because of the remarkable things achieved by using hypnosis. To illustrate this point and to try to understand where Tony was at, I recall a mate of Peter McKay from Sunderland who was an ambulance driver by profession, but also did the clubs circuit as a performing hypnotist. He was so good that he could implant a trigger word into someone's mind whilst they were under his hypnotic spell, and any time he spoke that 'key' word the person would respond immediately.

They say that under hypnosis one cannot do what one does not wish to do. This may be so in trivial matters like pretending to be a ballet dancer or standing on your head at the given unconscious demand. However, in one case, Peter's hypnotist friend was talking to a mate of his in the control room of his particular ambulance station over the ambulance radio. As they were chatting, a key of trigger word was used and the man in the control centre could not let go of the phone no matter how hard he tried.

This same hypnotist had another experience that disturbed him so much that he nearly gave it all up. He was working, I believe, in a club somewhere in Sunderland. As usual, he got someone from the audience to help in the demonstration. This unfortunate but willing victim was made to lie on the floor and be hypnotised into becoming as stiff as a board. Other volunteers were brought up and asked to lift this human-log between two chairs, his head resting on one chair, his feet resting on the other. Suddenly - and the hypnotist was never sure why - he told his stiff volunteer to float. As he told him to float he took away one chair. The man remained horizontal. While still telling the man to float he then took away the other chair. The man was now floating in mid air.

The audience went wild. They loved it, but they thought it was a trick! Quickly, the hypnotist put back the chairs, lifted his spell and the man went back to his seat. The hypnotist hurriedly finished his act and went back to his dressing room where he was found in a cold sweat trembling. "Did you see what I did? How did I do it? That man was bloody floating!" So it was easy to see how a trick or two like that could make a man think that he was in fact someone rather special, even, as in Tony's case, Jesus.

I asked Tony to prove to me that he was Jesus. "What was the group of men called who taught Jesus and John the Baptist prior to his ministry?" I asked. Tony paused – "Hebrews". "Oh come on, you will have to do better than that" I said rather firmly, as this flippant answer was similar to the one concerning where Jung was born ("Out of my mother's womb"). I then asked Tony to explain to me the law of karma or of action and reaction. He replied that it was a man-made law and did not exist. "Who was the man in the black that I saw bending over you during the operation?" "There was no man in black," came the reply. I persisted; "Who was he?" "I cannot tell you," said Tony. "Why not?" I said. "I cannot." "You must." "It was the fallen one." "What on Earth was he doing there?" "When such operations are being performed he is always there to witness them." "Not in my book," I said.

"Look, I will demonstrate to you that I am Jesus," said Tony, standing up. He then stretched his arms up to the ceiling and contorted his face until he shook. I asked what that was supposed to prove. He made no reply. He then sat down beside me and asked me to feel the muscles tighten in his back. I did so reluctantly. I again asked what this proved. "I consider myself a relatively intelligent man," I told him "but you are insulting me. You have no power and nothing to say."

By now, he seemed almost desperate to prove to me that he was indeed someone special. "Watch the colour of my eyes change. Look into my eyes." He knelt before me. "Alright," I said "Your last chance." He made the shape of a pyramid with his two forefingers and thumbs. He uttered a small prayer intermingled with gibberish, then blew gently through the pyramid. I gazed into his blue eyes. "See, they are changing into brown," he said. His eyes remained blue. I believe I left him feeling rather frustrated and I have to confess I felt rather sad. I believe he genuinely wished to help me. I believe also that there was a genuine gift of healing, but his giant ego took over. He became an open door to outside entities.

I found out later that he had made a verbal pass at my lady friend whom I had sent to him for relaxation. She didn't want to tell me because she still hoped that he could help me and didn't want to destroy any confidence I might have had. This was a terrible breach of professional conduct.

I discovered that Blythe College, where Tony had apparently trained, was not recognised by the main professional body of hypnotherapists in London. Also, he was apparently married with children and had never done a stroke of work in his life. I, like so many people, respond to kindness. Tony never personally harmed me. For three months he did everything he could to help me and never asked for a penny. I heard eventually that he had gone to many healing centres, trying to muscle in. Most healers are sensitives; he was obviously under the influence of undesirables and was quietly asked to leave.

Perhaps I should have been more careful. Perhaps in some way I was responsible for his sudden psychic development, but his kindness blinded me even though I was suspicious. I understand these years later that he still maintains that he is Jesus. He runs a healing group and is surrounded by women and devotees, one of which bore his child. (No immaculate conception, I'll warrant). But he has done more harm than good. Many people are under his hypnotic spell. Many, I believe, have been mentally harmed and are now in a psychiatric hospital. He has been exposed by a Sunday newspaper, but is still practising. The police are aware of him and so are the churches, but at present they can do nothing for he has broken no laws, at least no physical laws.

I find all this very sad. But he is not the first nor will he be the last to be hoodwinked by that yapping dog ego and its accompanying disciples.

CHAPTER 12

*I*n the previous chapter, I briefly mentioned pyramid power. Some of you may be aware of the power of shape. In the case of the pyramid, the most publicised phenomena is its power to sharpen razor blades by stimulating and reproducing the crystalline structure of the blade. Also, seeds germinate much quicker inside a pyramid, providing the pyramid is made to the exact scale of the Great Pyramid of Giza, scaled down of course. Flowers grow at an extremely fast rate. Meat and vegetables dehydrate and are preserved without rotting.

I decided to hold an experiment of my own. I built an exact replica of the Great Pyramid, scaled down to about half a metre. I made it of polystyrene ceiling tiles. I placed it on a wooden board and put it in the middle of a three-metre square of garden, exactly on magnetic north as in the case of the Great Pyramid. I ran copper wire up the sides, over the apex and down, then out to the corners of my three-metre plot of garden. The wire then turned inwards, pointing towards the pyramid.

I then got my mother to plant vegetables in this marked plot, the same vegetables that she had planted further up the garden. As the weeks went by, the garden sprang into life, but not *my* plot. Things grew, but very, very slowly. The rest of the garden was flourishing, but by the beginning of July my little plot was way behind. I couldn't understand it. It was now near the end of July and I knew that my plot would never catch up. I pulled up the pyramid and the copper wire. Within a week the whole three-metre plot sprang into life!

Within another two weeks, the vegetables had almost caught up. Somehow the pyramid had retarded their growth. Inside, they flourished, outside they were stunted. One wonders about the pyramids of Egypt standing in the middle of a desert.

The power of the ancient stone circles that are dotted in various forms all over the country cannot, in my personal experience, be denied and I had always promised myself that I would visit Stonehenge (although Stonehenge now is almost dead, the energy lines blocked).

On my first visit to Glastonbury, I stopped off with Geoff Edenborough, a friend of my father, to look at Stonehenge, this historic site steeped in mystery and mystical mayhem. Like so many people, we were disappointed that it was so small. Strangely, I felt nothing significant there. Even tuning in brought a negative response. But it was peaceful. I sensed no anger, only age.

Years later, I visited the Avebury Stones. I was with Peta, a girlfriend of mine, who I was taking to Glastonbury to work temporarily for a small spiritual group. On the way, we diverted to Avebury. The stones started to loom large and lovely as we entered the village. We stopped by the side of the road and parked. On the right hand side of the road, with the main part of the village right in front, stood huge, enormous, awe-inspiring stones. Why they impressed me more than Stonehenge at first sight, I'm not really sure. We opened a small gate and walked towards them. I had the odd sensation of power, difficult to describe. I needed very little tuning in. My channel was already opening. I made towards the largest stone and placed my hands on it. I felt no direct force from the stone, but my mind felt somewhat numb.

I started to walk around the stone. It was extraordinary. I felt as though I was wading through water. It was difficult to walk without effort. "You are walking round anti-clockwise. The power spirals clockwise" said Peta suddenly. I immediately changed direction and it was much easier. Peta was right. The incredible earth power (linked to the Earth's 'Telluric grid') was spiralling clockwise, but what I also became very aware of was the fact that the power was neutral, neither negative or positive. ('Telluric' means to flow in and out. The Telluric power lines carry both healing lines and 'courier' lines, plus male and female energy, or ch'i.) It was just a huge column of spiralling power. But for what? How was it used? I have a theory (yes, I know, another theory) that, like a piece of quartz crystal when a small current is passed through it, the power is amplified. Similarly the crystalline structure of certain rocks could possibly amplify this natural vortex of spiralling earth power.

I recently discovered a clue to the power's use. An architect friend of mine, Malcolm Murdock, was asked whether he was interested in an experiment involving a certain technique that can stimulate the memory of the unconscious. That is, that part of the unconscious that is hooked into the akashic record, the indelible record of events since time began. This technique is in itself very simple. The recipient is asked to lie down, after first removing his shoes, and relax totally whilst his or her forehead and feet are massaged in a certain way. Whilst this is being done, the recipient relaxes even more. Then they are asked to imagine that they are floating up through the roof, up and up, then come down to the ground outside the house. At this stage they are asked to describe what they see. What Malcolm experienced was beyond anything he could imagine.

He suddenly found himself dressed as a Druid priest all in white. He carried a long staff, the head of which resembled two spirals. He was standing beside a huge monolith. Around him were many other standing stones. Outside of this seeming stone circle he could see people clustering around open fires. The ground he stood on was stamped down through years of use. As he looked down the avenue of stones, he saw huge prehistoric monsters, then Roman soldiers, and finally modern day tanks. The one thing that stuck out in his mind was that the Moon was in the stone, not above, not shining on it, but IN it (the Moon's phases have a great effect on the power of stone megaliths). He could not explain to me why.

The interesting point here is the symbol of two spirals, which obviously illustrate the spiralling power (or double helix) of the stones. Could it be that Malcolm, in a previous life, was a Druid priest? That he was also a clairvoyant, which enabled him to see the past, present and future? If this stone complex he saw was Stonehenge, then it is reasonable to suppose that he would see the prehistoric monsters that once roamed Ancient Britain, depicting the past. The Roman soldiers who tried to get rid of the Druids were also based at Salisbury and depicted the present (during that time). Finally, the modern day tanks depicted the war games now acted out by the British Army on Salisbury Plain.

It is my theory that Malcolm tapped the power of the stones to heighten his powers of clairvoyance. It is, after all, a neutral power and needs to be channelled. Perhaps even the power of thought (telepathy) could be amplified and received thousands of miles away by a similar priest in a similar location? (More of this in later chapters.)

The Moon being in the stone I am not sure about, only that the Moon goddess is symbolised by a spiral and the power of the stone spirals. I believe there has to be a connection. (I should say at this point that Malcolm never had an interest in Druidism or ancient standing stones. He expressed a passing interest in archaeology and Egyptology, but that was all. What happened to him came as a complete surprise. He didn't think anything would happen at all and when it did he could hardly believe what he saw.)

Which brings me swiftly on to the subject of Leucathea, the white goddess, the Moon goddess. For many years I have been fascinated by the Moon, so much so that in order to sleep sometimes I imagine I climb some sort of spacecraft and fly to the Moon. Sometimes I land, sometimes I don't. Also, on one occasion, I have found myself spouting poetry at the Moon ad lib, inspired by God knows what.

Ten years ago, I was given a walking stick as a present by a river bailiff for my work as a poet. He found it in a raw state in the River Stour, near Canterbury. He shaped the head, though nature had done most of the work for him, like a fox or dog. I had to trim it here and there and finally varnished it. It is a beautiful stick and wherever I go it attracts admirers.

A year or so ago I happened upon a book by Colin Wilson, called *The Occult*. In it I discovered information concerning the cult of the Moon taken from a book written by the late Robert Graves, called *The White Goddess*. I was so taken by what I learned that I purchased a copy for myself. In this very difficult book, I found that the white goddess, also known as the triple headed goddess of birth, death and rebirth, is the goddess of poetic inspiration and the subconscious. Among her symbols are a roebuck or stag, a thicket, and a crescent Moon.

I learned also from the book that a spiral was also heavily regarded throughout the ages as a representative of the triple headed goddess (the Moon in the stone? The spiralling at Avebury?). Her sacred tree was the alder or willow. My stick is made of alder. The poet is forever fascinated by women; whoever the poet falls in love with, the goddess resides in her. I have had a life-long fascination with womankind and certainly most of those who have touched my life were drawn to me by poetry, either theirs or my own. First and foremost, I am a poet. From the age of 21 (my third cycle), the power of poetry, the white goddess, obsessed me. I do not consider myself a particularly good poet, but that is really what most people remember me as ("Oh yes, you're Paul Bura the poet aren't you?").

In 1985 I went to Gambia for a holiday. Whilst there, I discovered that the power of the 'juju' was as widespread as it ever was and I was anxious to meet a genuine juju man. The juju man, or malibu, is the local medicine man and caster of spells. He is held in high esteem. Most of the folk in Gambia wear some sort of amulet charged by the malibu to protect him or her from being beaten, stabbed, shot or some other physical or psychic attack. Of course, it is reasonable to say that because the malibu and the power of the juju is so respected and feared, only a fool would attack someone wearing a protective belt or wrist band empowered with the juju, so one would assume that it was fear that was the protector and not the juju.

However, I have to relate the story of the white man who drove his jeep through a village in West Africa and was stopped from driving any further by the villagers and their malibu. The malibu told the white man that he must turn around and find another route, as he was about to drive through sacred ground. The white man decided in his arrogance that no matter what, he was going to drive through. The malibu, without touching the jeep whatsoever, told the white man that he could no longer start his jeep and it was pointless him trying until he agreed to turn round.

The white man tried to start the jeep – he couldn't. He tried again – still the jeep wouldn't start. He tried for about 10 minutes and then in resignation born of frustration he agreed to change his route and go around the sacred ground. The malibu then told him he could now start his vehicle. The jeep started at the first touch, much to the utter amazement of the driver. This then, is just part of the power of the juju.

We befriended one of the security guards at the hotel called Kaleef. He agreed to take me to meet a genuine malibu, for there are many in West Africa, some better than others. We enjoyed a wonderful day out to Senegal and then back to Kaleef's village where we shared and enjoyed a communal bowl of what seemed like toasted ground maize with sugar and evaporated milk. The bowl was placed on a rather rickety table and we three, John Webster, myself and Kaleef, armed with a spoon each, tucked in. Soon we were off again. We sped through more villages, throwing up great clouds of red dust that literally covered my white smock and trousers in a red indelible haze. Children were everywhere and so, so beautiful. They never asked for money, only pens. The more pens you owned the more important you were. Pens were not provided at village schools. (If you ever go to Gambia, take a box of biros.)

Kaleef directed us to a walled white house. Outside, sitting in the dust, were three old men. As we approached, one of them got up and went inside. Kaleef was silent. He ushered us into a small courtyard, up some small steps where we entered the small brick house. The malibu greeted Kaleef, who looked at him nervously, then showed us into a small room dominated by a huge canopied double bed covered by a multi-coloured counterpane. The malibu, whose name was Dramah – he was of the Mandingo tribe – indicated that we should sit down. He squatted on the floor, his back to the bed. To his left were strewn many scrolls with strange designs and writings on them. There were also many bottles containing I know not what – medicines of some kind? - plus the odd empty gin and cola bottle. He reminded me of the Mahatma Ghandi on a bad day, except that he wore more clothes. He asked through Kaleef what it was that I wanted. I told him that I wanted my stick (the stick of the goddess) to be charged. The malibu shook his head and pointed to a mass of belts and bracelets that were already charged. I told him, whilst Kaleef interpreted, that I was not interested in them, that it was important to me that my stick be charged. He finally agreed but requested £50 for the job. I knocked him down to £10, knowing that this was the custom. A £10 note in the Gambia returns a high rate of exchange.

I asked him if he ever used the power of the Moon. He said that, on occasion, he did, but only under Allah. This pleased me. He still believed in one supreme God and the Moon goddess was but an expression of the Infinite. He needed to keep my stick for a night. He also required a little more money (about 50p) as a payment to the leather craftsman who would seal the magic objects with wet leather on to the surface of The Riverman

(I call the stick 'The Riverman' after the bailiff who gave it to me). I have no idea what these objects are, but I can feel them under their leather seal. When we left the malibu's house, Kaleef was visibly shaken and immediately asked John for a cigarette. I think there was no doubt in my mind that we had met a man of power, a genuine malibu or juju man.

The stick was delivered the next day. I cannot honestly say it felt any different, but woe betide anyone who tries to steal it.

(Robert Graves states that the cult of the moon goddess, *Ngame*, started in West Africa. Odd that I should go there.)

CHAPTER 13

*B*eing an actor and writer is not exactly the best way to earn a living and being disabled didn't exactly help matters, so I very often buried myself in voluntary social work. Once a week, for nearly eight years, I visited Jim Redding, a victim of multiple sclerosis. 'Jim' and his wife 'Anne' (these are not their real names) became close friends and I became somewhat part of the family. Jim is a very intelligent and articulate man and we spent many hours locked in conversation. Sometimes, with the help of my mate, John Webster, we loaded up his wheelchair in the car and took him to the pictures.

Jim's wife, Anne, was an artist whose original works were reproduced and sold all over the world. She looked after Jim as best she could, but sometimes it was necessary for one such as I to take the load off. I occasionally gave Jim a little spiritual healing. My gift is small, but with multiple sclerosis anything is worth a try. I wasn't able to help him physically, but socially we enjoyed one another. Conversation ranged from the women in our lives to religion. We also touched on my interest on psychic matters. Jim neither believed nor disbelieved, but he listened knowing (I think), that I was not a complete fool.

It was during one of our conversations that Anne produced a brass ship propeller. It was obviously from a model because it was only 3" long. "Paul, do you think you might do a psychometry on this and tell me what you see?" I said that I would have a go, but, as usual, could promise nothing. I cleared my head and tuned in, holding the brass object firmly in my hands. The first thing I saw was clouds blowing very quickly across the sun as if time were suddenly speeded up and days were flashing by. Then I saw Anne standing in front of a very ornate glass topped table in a beautifully furnished room with long drapes.

Standing behind her was a rather tallish, very dark, good looking man who was putting a thick gold chain around her neck. At this point of my reading I heard Anne gasp. I paused, then carried on. Suddenly I saw a huge explosion. Anne again gasped. The reading was at an end. I opened my eyes and asked what Anne had seen. "You saw a man that I once knew who was to have given me that gold necklace, but he died in an explosion during the war." "How did the propeller come into it?" I asked. "It was in the building where he died during the blitz," she said simply. Anne looked at me steadily. "Who did you think it was?" she said. Into my head came the name "Al Bowly". I dismissed it as ridiculous. "I don't know," I said.

The next week I visited as usual. Jim asked me if I would do him a favour. It was Anne's birthday next week and he wanted me to buy an Al

Bowly album for her. I swallowed hard. I managed to get the album without any trouble. There had been a distinct revival of 1930's big bands, including Lou Stone, Henry Hall, and Paul Whiteman, and Al Bowly - a singer - was a very big name indeed. I gave the album to Jim, whiled away an hour in conversation, and then I was off home.

The following week I went to see Jim. Anne was out and Jim was not looking his usual self. "Paul I have got something to tell you that I can tell nobody else and I would appreciate it if what I tell you remains for now between you and me". "Yes, of course," I said. "You bought that Al Bowly record for Anne, didn't you?" "Yes" I said. "Well the other day we played it for the first time. Directly Al started to sing Anne's eyes seemed to take on a strange look. I had never seen her look like that before and then came the strangest thing of all - she started to take all her clothes off. I asked her what she was doing. She didn't answer me. She then lay down on the floor and I swear to you Paul, someone was making love to my wife. We have been married for well over 30 years and I know when my wife is being made love to." "Well, who was it?" I asked very curiously. "You are not going to believe this, but I have just discovered that Anne was married to Al Bowly before she married me *(in the 1930's when Anne was only 16, she had managed to get the last ticket for a Duke Ellington concert at the Trocadero Theatre in the Elephant and Castle. When she took her seat she found she was sitting next to Al Bowly. It was then the affair started)* and she swears the person who was making love to her was Al. What do you make of that?" When Jim told me the tale, I told him that I had received the name Al Bowly in my vision and that "the man I saw standing behind Anne was Al Bowly."

I told him that I had heard of the odd husband who had come back if the link was strong enough and made love to their wives after passing, but it was very rare. Besides, not many people would dare admit to such a thing for fear of ridicule, which would make it seemingly rarer still.

At this point Anne arrived back. They had obviously discussed the possibility of telling me, because Anne sat down and joined in the conversation. She told me that after the incident where Al had made love to her, she would wake in the morning to find that her telephone notepad was covered in Al's writing. "I'm afraid it is very crude," she said. "Al was a virile man and making love was to him like having a drink. He could make love 10 times a day; he was obsessed by sex."

It seemed that he used her at night during her sleep state to do automatic writing. Anne showed me one of his original letters to her, that she had kept. He always referred to her as "Baby". She then showed me his latest writing, using her as a medium. It was identical. (Anne had apparently destroyed all Al's letters and gramophone records when he died and blocked him from her mind, blocked him so totally that never a word of him ever reached Jim.) The letters were indeed highly sexual.

At this juncture, one must state that Jim and Anne could not now have normal sexual relations because of Jim's M.S. so one could well believe that this was a fantasy conjured up by a childhood crush on a very popular 30's singer, resulting in this rather bizarre episode. But Al was not the only communicator to write through Anne. She also began to find the writings of Tony Bramley in the morning, an old homosexual friend of hers whom she knew during the same period. He lived in Eton Place at the time.

Not only that, but Jim also was aware that Al was in the house, that he actually sat down and watched television with them. I asked Anne what she wanted to do about it. She said that she just didn't know. She knew she could shut him off from her if she wanted to, but as Jim seemed to have accepted the situation (and Jim would do anything for Anne) she thought she would let it ride for the time being.

After a week or so, I noticed that things between Jim and Anne were not quite what they should be. I think Jim was just a little jealous of finding a disembodied Al Bowly around the place messing around with his wife. Anne too, I think, was nearing the end of her tether. There was a lot of tension and what with Jim's physical problems and day to day routine this was not at all surprising.

I suggested that maybe I try to contact Al and find out what he wanted (although I suppose it was pretty obvious what he wanted). I suggested that I write a kind of questionnaire, leaving gaps for Al to answer, to be placed by Anne's bed. Anne and Jim agreed. I typed out a few questions, such as: "Since you died have you seen or been approached by anyone?" "Can you replay or relive highlights of your life?" "Do you want to go further over instead of staying in the in-between world? If so I might be able to help."

Al ignored my piece of typed paper, but wrote instead on the phone pad. Yes, he could watch the highlights of his life, sexual and professional, any time he wanted. If he wanted to wear a certain suit of clothes, he only had to think of them and they were there. Time flew by so quickly when he slept. Days went by like seconds, weeks like minutes, and years like months (hence my vision of time flashing by). He had seen no-one since he came there and was quite happy as he was, providing he could still have his 'Baby' (he pronounced Baby "Babee"). Anne decided to block him off again. This she did quite successfully.

However, a few months later I was being interviewed by Frank Whoppett on Radio Newcastle concerning my latest book of poems. Now

Frank had gone with a friend to see a medium years before and Al Bowly had apparently been standing near him. Frank was a great Al Bowly fan and later he formed the Al Bowly Appreciation Society with members all over the world. He played Al's records on radio at the drop of a needle. There is always an Al Bowly record squeezed in somewhere on his show. After telling Frank briefly, without naming names, what had taken place he said the bit he didn't quite understand was Anne's marriage to Al. Frank said there was no record of this. Al had been married, but not to Anne.

When I returned to Kent I put this to Anne. She said that he had married her last, but under another name - the name of Al's mother who was Lebanese - and for the life of her she could not remember it. She was, after all, only 16 when they met and he was in his late 30's. She married at 19. After the marriage, things began to fall apart. His sexual preferences became bizarre and his cocaine habit didn't help matters. They drifted further and further apart. The next she heard was that he had been killed in an explosion during the blitz. It was said that he was sitting up in bed reading when this happened. Anne said this was utter nonsense. Apart from the odd comic he never read a book in his life!

Although Al had made love to her in front of Jim she had only ever 'seen' him once. She was walking her dog on the beach near Hampton Pier in Herne Bay, when she saw Al, as large as life, sitting on an upturned boat. "He looked as solid as you or I," said Anne. He smiled and was gone. (Water is a great source of power.)

There has been no recurrence of Al Bowly in their lives since, but he has certainly been active around me. Soon after these happenings concerning Jim and Anne had ceased, I was telling Debbie Cork, a friend of mine who had come to spend the evening with me, the whole story, making sure, of course, that this was in complete confidence. After finishing the tale I put on a cassette of Al singing. The door suddenly blew open - Debbie nearly had a heart attack. There was no wind that night.

Years later I was at Sands Wine Bar in Ramsgate. Friends of mine had just bought it and the place was jammed-packed. Music was thumping out from two speakers set up on top of a shelf over a large wine rack. For some reason I found myself telling the Al Bowly story to my old friend, Chris Goldthorpe. I was having to yell in his ear to make myself heard and certainly no-one else could have listened to what I was saying. Suddenly, there was a crash. One of the speakers at the far end of the bar had crashed to the floor. After the initial silence, the babble of 150 people took over again and I went on with the story. Within a few minutes of the first speaker falling from the shelf, the second speaker crashed down, hitting one of the bar girls on the shoulder. Coincidence?

I asked Richard, who had just sold the wine bar and who was helping out on that particular night, whether those speakers had fallen off the shelf before. He said never. The music was no louder than it had been when he ran the Sands and he could not understand how it had happened. I suggested that the wine rack had more wine in it than usual and therefore had bent the shelf lower than normal, and coupled with the sound... Richard denied this – the rack held the same amount of wine as usual.

Did Al object to my telling the story of his sexual exploits? I am not sure. But I do believe that it is Al's obsession with sex that is holding him so close to the Earth, and until he realises that, he is going to be hanging about getting bored for centuries. His 'Baby' eventually died in her late sixties. Jim went into a residential home in Herne Bay. Jim is the first person who you'll meet there as he now works in reception. He is not the sort to vegetate. No sir!

CHAPTER 14

*E*arly in the writing of this book, I was interrupted by a phone call from Amy, a friend of mine from Washington, Tyne and Wear. She was being troubled by (as far as I could make out) the disembodied spirit of her brother-in-law who had committed suicide three weeks before. Following my suggestion, Amy had tried talking to Alec, telling him that he must look around him, call for help, search for a lighted doorway and then help would be given. He would be taken to a place where he could rest and get his spiritual breath.

Alternately, he should tune in to Amy and her surroundings, clothing her with light and energy and asking for nothing save the power of love to help him in his dilemma. For about two days, Amy coped and accepted that he was following her about the house. The smell of after-shave always preceded him. Amy needed reassuring that she was not going mad. A friend of hers called in. She too could smell this powerful after-shave.

Amy phoned again. This time she was really shaken. He had apparently put his hands on her shoulders as she was preparing for bed. She could handle it by day, but not at night, especially with three children aged between 10 and seven in the house. She could not take it any longer.

I suggested she get in touch with some friends of ours in Sunderland who, in turn, would get hold of Canon Stock to see if he would perform a service of exorcism, and by doing so help this unfortunate soul in his premature migration to the other world.

The call was made. Father Stock was willing, but there was a lot of ecclesiastical red tape to be got over before the exorcism could take place. The Bishop must be consulted. Canon Stock could not step on the toes of any authorised church-recognised practising exorcist. I could not believe this. Here was a lady being pursued in her own home and indeed to her own local swimming bath where she was suddenly overwhelmed by the pungent smell of the after-shave over the smell of the chlorine. This lady needed help now, not tomorrow or next week.

Kay Wood, a wonderful lady full of light and wisdom, and a close friend of mine, suggested I get in touch with Malcolm Date, a qualified osteopath and healer who also dealt with the laying of spirits. I realised, after phoning him, that we had spoken before concerning the Tony Vernon-Vaughn episode, so it was good to know I had a friendly ally. I briefly told Malcolm what had taken place and he agreed to help. I then phoned Amy, who in turn phoned Malcolm.

As is usual in these matters, Malcolm needed something that belonged to Amy, so she wrote him a brief note. By physical contact (though sometimes the sound of the voice will do), with this note Malcolm would be able to give out a cleansing energy and one that would keep the unhappy Earth-bound person out of Amy's way. Although Alec was scared and disorientated through not being able to talk to anybody, Amy was now in a state of terror. Her mother came to stay with her for a night or two, but even with a stiff drink inside her, sleep was almost impossible.

Up until then I had been 'sending out' to Amy, but with little success. Malcolm was not too happy about the church being called in. In his experience, it can sometimes make things worse. The very presence of a priest or exorcist can leave a part of one's self (one's personality) in the place that is being exorcised and this can get in the way of the purifying power of the light. Malcolm has found that exorcism is very often more effective if practised at a distance. Amy sent her letter on a Saturday morning, first class, so Malcolm would in all probability get it Monday morning.

On that Monday afternoon, Amy was just dozing off in sheer exhaustion when she was woken by a loud noise, like a sharp crack or crash. Amy told me "I must have shot two feet in the air, my nerves were in such a state." She searched around, but could find no cause for this noise. After that, peace reigned once more. It was as though a great surge of psychic energy was focused on Amy and her house, resulting in that startling noise almost like the great static electrical charges that end in a gigantic thunderclap. That surge of psychic energy brought harmony again to a lady who, for nearly a week, was more scared than she had ever been in her life - and who could blame her?

Later, Amy's husband, brother of Alec, was going through Alec's things when he came across a bottle of after-shave. He showed the after-shave to Amy. One smell was all it took to send it hurtling into the dustbin!

CHAPTER 15

*I*n 1979, I started recording *Sounds, Words and Movement* for BBC Radio 4 (Schools). It was my first job as a children's presenter and my producer then was Vera Gray. I had auditioned for light entertainment a few months before at Broadcasting House and forgotten all about it. I was doing the ironing when the phone rang. It was Vera, offering me my first 'Beeb' (BBC) series. The money wasn't all that good, but then it never is at the Beeb. I was speechless with joy. It was just before Christmas and I had been having a very lean time of it. I was to start on February 7th, 1979.

Vera Gray had apparently been looking (or listening) for a new male voice. She had spent hours listening to audition tapes, but the voice she sought didn't make itself heard. Apparently the engineer who had recorded my audition remembered me and suggested Vera had a listen - and that launched me into five good years at Broadcasting House.

Vera Gray was like working with one's favourite aunt. The whole team were like a family and Vera looked after us. Musicians, actors, studio managers, and grams operators, all were warm under her wing.

During this time, I started having yet another recurring dream. This was the classic actor's dream of being on stage, but not having learnt one line of the play. Mine was different in that, although terrified that I had not learnt my lines, I was actually going on stage and *reading* my part from the script. Six months before, I had written to *The Stage*, the actors' periodical, asking about actors who had become wheelchair bound, either due to being paralysed from the waist down (paraplegics), having legs crushed in car accidents, or, as in my case, through polio.

Why was it we could not get work in radio when the government had already passed a Bill where it was compulsory for big companies to employ 5% of disabled people? I don't just mean lift operators. Naturally, one would only be employed if one had talent, not just employment on compassionate grounds. I received a reply from an independent producer, one Trevor Handoll. He thought it might be a good idea if we met. I agreed and from that meeting was born the idea of putting on a play with half professional crippled actors and the other half 'normal' actors. During the summer of 1979 a script arrived. It was a play by Martin George (Trevor Handoll) called *The Last Trial of Mrs M*, the story of Kate Merrick, the 1920s club owner. I was to play the prosecutor. The part was bigger than Hamlet! My stomach turned over. Already I was terrified. My family supported me, especially my sister Mellie, and with great trepidation I hauled myself and a lead-heavy script up to London to start rehearsals.

It was to be an off-West End production at the Janetta Cochrane Theatre. The first day of rehearsals was sheer hell for me. My mind was like marble and would not absorb the lines. I was nearly in tears. If it wasn't for our leading lady, Mary Wilson, I think I would have thrown in the towel. I was on stage all the time, seated high up in my prosecutor's wig and gown. Mary persuaded me that I could do it. And I did do it, but not in the time-honoured tradition. You see, as I was playing the prosecutor I therefore had to carry a bundle of notes, so why shouldn't it be the script? I learned all the major speeches, well, most of them, and the reassurance of having my text for instant referral carried me through. The dream then came true.

The rest of the production was a triumph in itself. By clever seating and lighting, by the fitting of small wheels on the back legs of chairs, non-walking actors were moved from one scene to another and for a whole week we fooled the public and the press into thinking we were an ordinary company of actors putting on yet another play.

However, I was never really happy in the production, mainly because I knew I was cheating, and I was glad when our short run ended.

CHAPTER 16

I have always been fascinated by trees. If I see a huge lone tree high up on a hill I mentally greet it, at the same time regretting that I cannot run to it and fling my arms around it. I believe that a tree not only lives, but is highly conscious, that certain trees and plants give off an aura of power and healing. I believe that trees are tuned into the realms of nature and know oneness as an every day event. My 1987 book *The Oak on the Plain* related to this fantastic reality.

I was sitting meditating one day with a group of friends, when my consciousness began to expand and in my mind I saw a huge, beautiful tree. Not only did I see the tree, but I became the tree. I knew what it was to have the wind blow through me and how wonderful and refreshing wind could be. I knew what it was to have rain fall on me, birds nest in me, insects feed from me, how many leaves would fall from me and would be sucked into the earth, revitalised so that I could take that sustenance back up through my roots.

I knew also the pain of the axe, though it was more a mental pain, a kind of disharmony, not physical pain as we know it, but pain nonetheless. Over and above all this was the knowledge that I was aware of every tree about me. I knew every one by name, even those at the edge of the forest that I could not see. The communication with my fellows, even the grass that grew below me, was such a wonderful thing and wisdom grew in me without effort.

This experience is common enough amongst those far more in tune than I, but this glimpse will stay with me always.

After my parents' divorce I didn't see my father for 14 years. We heard rumours that he had gone back into the old family business of fried fish and chips (my father was the first man to sell crinkly chips commercially. He also helped to invent and build the old penny-operated slot machine Steer-a-Ball. Not a lot of people know that!). He ended up working in maintenance as an engineer for a hospital in Southend.

A mutual friend suggested that I might like to see him again. Dad was coming to Herne Bay for a small visit. I agreed to meet him at the friend's house, together with his two children, Saul and Linda (my half

Us kids: Melvina, me and Kevin sitting on Josie's lap.

brother and sister). Dad opened the door and I hugged and kissed him (us Buras do a lot of that -it must be the thespian in us). His hair was now iron grey and 14 years on, time was etched firmly onto his face. I asked him how he was, how his new family were. He spoke of nothing but himself and his problems.

At first, this was fine because a lot can happen in 14 years, but after an hour he was still on the same track. My father had not progressed as a person one iota. He was still the same rather selfish man that I had always known. He never once asked me how I was, how Mellie was, how Josie and Kev were. He mentioned our mother once briefly, but that was all. Life had been cruel to him and had dealt him too many blows. It all sounded like an excuse for his behaviour towards us, his first family, a way of saying "I might have let you all down, but I am suffering for it."

As a child I loved and respected my father. He was a good father and a great craftsman. There was nothing he could not make or build if he put his mind to it. He taught me how to use tools and how to appreciate them. I do not think he understood me as a growing adult. I somehow grew away from him, and his affair finally pulled the shutter down until the meeting 14 years on. The shutter lifted briefly, but little light shone through, and slowly it came down again.

My father died of cancer in 1985. An old friend of his from way back informed me: "Joe is dead." "Who?" I said. He answered "Your father, Joe. He died last night." I thanked him for telling me. I didn't even know Dad was ill. There had been no word that he was poorly, no message from his other family (though perhaps they didn't realise how ill he was). I felt very little. I wish I had felt more, but I didn't.

That night (Saturday) I went to see my journalist friend, John Webster. For once, instead of rock and roll on the stereo he was playing Vivaldi's *Four Seasons*. I sat back, allowing the music to fill me and set me flying with its incredible power and beauty. Suddenly, I was aware of my father kneeling beside me (that is, sitting on his haunches – a physical idiosyncrasy of his). He had come to say goodbye. He asked also that I should forgive him for any pain that he might have caused. He genuinely thought he had been misunderstood. I told him that there was nothing to forgive, that I only wished I could have loved him more. I wished him well and told him I bore no malice, that there was no hate in my heart; that he should go with God to the next stage of his journey. It was as simple as that. John was aware of nothing – only Vivaldi.

CHAPTER 17

*O*ne psychic experience, one that was almost complete in its coming together aspect, was a story that started in a small recording studio in Ashford, Kent. Bernard Shaw has been a friend of mine for many years and we have worked together many times doing commercial voice-overs and film commentaries. Bernard is essentially a musician and composer. As a percussionist, he had worked with some of the best orchestras in England. He is articulate and very bright, a very compassionate soul, but also somewhat of a cynic in as much as he will not accept anything unless he has investigated it thoroughly and completely and even then will still retain an open mind; a quality that I admire.

Bernie and I had talked many times about the paranormal, but in particular about spiritual matters, the Universal Oneness, the golden thread that runs through all the major religions. Bernie neither believed nor disbelieved, but events in his life brought about by great pain and emotional upset had gradually bent his stubborn way of thinking. Things were beginning to happen in his life that he could no longer push away, one being the experience of leaving his body after he was involved in a car crash. He observed, from some point above his crashed car, people crowding around the vehicle. He had the sensation that it was really nothing to do with him and wondered what all the fuss was about. The next thing he knew was coming to in his car and experiencing the pain. Bernie was not badly hurt, but the experience stayed with him though he was still very sceptical about it.

Bernard's studio in Ashford is small but welcoming. A slight smell of damp greets you after descending the stone steps to the basement, but it is warm and friendly. The recording session was booked for 10.00am and Bernie had asked me to be there a little earlier so that he could set up, get a voice level etc, so that we would be ready for the client when he arrived. The client arrived some 15 minutes late and, as is usual in the recording world, some minor alterations were made to the script before we could proceed. An hour and a half later, a delighted client left the studio clutching his now completed tape. I stayed behind to enjoy a cup of tea and to chat about the rather appalling script we had just ploughed through, but recognising that it was, after all, a living and one, though precarious, we enjoyed enormously.

"Something strange happened to me the other night," said Bernie. "Oh yeah, what was she like?" I quipped. "No, no, seriously," said Bernie, "I don't know if I told you, but the BBC in Scotland commissioned me to write and record some music for some children's poems. They sent me a tape of this lady reading the stuff. I was intrigued and very moved by the poems and the wonderful way in which the lady read them. Anyway, the other night I sat down to work on the score. I was using the synthesiser and was recording as I went. I had just got what I considered a good melody line going when I heard this voice say..." "Wait a minute," I said "what voice?" "I don't know what voice, but he told me I hadn't got it quite right. So I tried something else. "That's better," the voice said, "that's much better." This seemed to go on for hours and by the early morning I had finished it. The thing is, when I played it back I was amazed at what I heard. I don't remember writing three-quarters of it and though I say so myself it was very good and exactly fitted the mood of the poems."

By the time Bernie had finished telling me his story I was starting to get my psychic spine tingle. Clairvoyantly, I was beginning to see a man dressed in black velvet, wearing a three cornered hat and buckle shoes. He also had long white or fair hair. Bernie shrugged at the description and was as puzzled as I was. I asked him who wrote the poems and he said "Robert Louis Stevenson". *"Treasure Island!"* I cried excitedly. "The same period as the man I saw. What did Robert Louis Stevenson look like?" "No idea" said Bernie. "Interesting though."

The BBC apparently loved what Bernie had composed (or thought he had composed) and asked him to go to Scotland for a press call. He said he would be delighted, but could he meet the lady who had recorded the poems? The BBC said they would do their best to get her there.

Two weeks later, I was again working with Bernie and after the session we got talking about the Robert Louis Stevenson affair. "So what happened in Scotland?" I asked. "Curiouser and curiouser" said Bernie. "I arrived at the press call as arranged and suddenly there she was, the lady who recorded the poems. She was dressed rather like a gypsy and I mean that in the nicest way. Her name was Harriet Buchan (she later played the sister of the TV character and series *Taggart*), a Scottish actress and we got on immediately. I told her that I was really inspired by her reading of Robert Louis Stevenson's work and she told me that the music I had written was exactly right and fitted her mood perfectly."

"She also said that we knew each other, didn't we? I told her that I knew what she meant. We had three minutes together and then she was gone. However, I have unearthed some information that might interest you concerning the background of RLS." "Have you now? Like what?" I said. "Well, a friend of mine did some research and it seems that RLS was interested in spiritual things like reincarnation, had an odd taste for Georgian costume and for stories set in that period. In his dreams he would find himself masquerading in - and you will like this bit - a three cornered hat, and was very much engaged in Jacobite conspiracy from the time his head hit the pillow at night until he woke up. He habitually wore a black velvet jacket and was nicknamed by various girlfriends as 'velvet coat'."

I realised then that I had seen truly. I had apparently picked up a conglomerate picture of RLS, but I still didn't know what he really looked like, whether he had long hair for instance. Did he write or compose music? But Bernie's side of the story was not yet complete.

"Now I am going to tell you something that really ties it all up. Have you any idea where the poems were recorded?" "None whatever," I replied. "They were recorded in the garden of a converted monastery that was once owned by - you have guessed it - Robert Louis Stevenson!"

There was only one loose end now – RLS's interest in music. Did he have any interest in music at all? The last and final part of the tale came to light a week later.

An employee of my partner and I – she worked next door to our health shop in the health 'studio', you know the sort of thing, gym, sauna, steam room, Jacuzzi – came into the shop. We got talking and she happened to mention that she was reading a biography of Robert Louis Stevenson. I started to ask her questions about RLS, but as she had only got about a quarter of the way through she could not really tell me what I wanted to know. To cut a long story short, she lent me the book. The book bore out everything I wanted to know. RLS always wore his hair long down to his shoulders; he was fascinated by the Georgian period; he did always wear a long black velvet jacket; his hair, however, was not fair or white, but brownish red, though I believe he did suffer from malaria which can turn the hair white.

At the age of 14, he wrote the words to an opera, a libretto, and one must come to the conclusion that to write a libretto he must have known the sort of music he wanted to accompany it, wouldn't you think?

CHAPTER 18

I was now entering my sixth seven-year cycle. I had no idea what it would bring. Perhaps again it would be two fold, some tragedy followed by enlightenment of some kind. Whatever it might bring, I knew that it could only grow in the process. I had learnt many things in my 42 years and there was much, much more yet to experience and understand. There was a void in me, even then, which only love and knowledge could fill.

One thing I knew then, as I do now, is that once you step on to your chosen path of seeming truth, no matter how crazy the paving, once you recognise the God within you, once you know that the true reality is the ability to love, then you are hooked and He will never let you go, no matter what horror or injustice you experience. The more you learn the more you realise how little you know. Though that can be analysed as intellectual one will never see God through the intellect.

Most intellectuals function only on facts, rejecting the ability to receive knowledge by inspiration from the higher self. People like Jung, Einstein, and Bronowski were, to my mind, exceptional human beings in that although they were intellectually brilliant, they did not reject that huge reservoir of creative thought that is beyond reason. They knew that it could burst the banks of the objective mind, bringing enlightenment to Mankind, most times not really knowing where it came from, but they recognised it and accepted it as truth from the Infinite, and with their exceptional intellect proved what they discovered by the scholarly gifts at their disposal. Truths came to them in a blinding flash on their inner screen and they knew instantly that they were so and then went on to prove them to their colleagues in the time-honoured way.

Someone once said that we come into this world with nothing and we leave with nothing. There is nothing further from the truth. What we can learn here on this weary, war-torn, yet beautiful planet, is worth far more than the ability to ship our material belongings into the next world.

The idea of bodily 'ascension', that is, the physical body actually disappearing, was, for a time, a great topic of so-called 'New Age' thought. To many people the idea is too outrageous and they dismiss it out of hand. Here then, I come to my good friend and fellow psychic, Malcolm Ing. The following story is perfectly true and happened about 25 years ago in the Medway town of Chatham, Kent. Malcolm, four other men and three women had been having regular weekly meetings for meditation and healing. On this occasion, on a warm June evening, there were no women for one reason or another. This left just the five men, including Malcolm. The invocation was given and the five men had just settled down to meditate, when one of the chairs was firmly pulled back by an unseen force. It was obvious to all that the gentleman occupying that seat was not meant to sit that evening. This was not a problem and he left. They settled down again.

From Malcolm's point of view this is what happened: He suddenly had a terrible urge to stand up, so he asked the man to his right if he thought it would be okay. The man said "Stand up." Malcolm was now standing in the middle of the small circle. He then said that he had a terrible urge to spin. Again, he was urged to do so. Malcolm found himself rising and turning and at the same time heard a great roar, like a jet plane going over head. The next thing he knew, he was lying on the floor!

Now, from the point of view of the other sitters, THIS is what happened: Malcolm and his opposite number, the man facing him, had both begun to gently pulse in unison. Malcolm stood up. He then rose very slightly off the floor and began to spin. From his mouth came a mighty roar... and then he completely and utterly disappeared! At that point, the man sitting opposite Malcolm stood up and pointed to a spot on the floor - blue static electricity rose from the spot indicated and curled up and around this man's arm. At that moment, Malcolm re-appeared lying on the floor! I assure you that this is perfectly true. Given this, and Joeb's (more of whom later) tales in later chapters of his Head Priest disappearing and re-appearing, the idea of bodily ascension takes on a greater reality.

CHAPTER 19

*I*n 1987, I started a new seven-year cycle. Peter and I sold our health food store in Herne Bay and went our different ways. Peter and his then lady, Rosemary, went into the wine bar business in the Midlands and I stayed on at the health store and worked part-time for the new owners until, six months later, I went to Australia to join my long-lost pal, John Webster, for a three-month trek around the land of Oz in an old VW Combie. John did the driving whilst I did the cooking. Australia to me is England, Scotland, Wales, Africa and all the tropics rolled into one. Every climate you can think of, every country you can think of, is there. And where do the Australians go for a holiday? They go to Hong Kong or Singapore!

For me though, the best part of the trip was when the Combie's engine blew up and we had to wait at least a week for a new one to be flown in from Brisbane to Cairns where we were holed up. Time was running out for me; I had to be back in Adelaide in three weeks to catch my plane back to Blighty. I made the decision to take a bus down through the Northern Territory to Alice Springs then on to Adelaide. I was now totally alone except for my suitcase and trusty wheelchair, which was handy for carrying the case, stopping me from falling over and providing me with a seat when I got tired. I won't dwell too long on the details of my journey other than to say that part of my quest in Australia was to track down a man called Dick Kimba.

Dick Kimba was an expert on the Australian Aborigines and had lived and worked with them for many years. The Aborigines had grown to love and respect this man and I suspected that he also knew some of their magical secrets. Arriving at Alice Springs at 5.30am (the driver was livid because he had just missed the first rainfall in Alice in two years!), I was greeted at my hotel by a very sleepy receptionist who had been waiting up for me, expecting a man with both legs in callipers and hardly able to walk. Boy, was she surprised and relieved to see that I could look after myself with the minimum of help.

The following day I started to phone around to

"You're not cold, are you?" John Webster and me as we travelled round Australia.

87

try to find Dick Kimba. I tried all the Aboriginal organisations, but drew a blank at each call. It seemed as if they were trying to protect his whereabouts, indeed even to deny that they knew him. At last, I was given the number of Dick's wife. It was her work number. She was very suspicious and wanted to know what I wanted with her husband. I explained that I was an English writer and broadcaster who was very interested in the Aborigines and needed to speak to someone in authority who had intimate dealings with these people. She paused. "I'll get back to you," she said. She took my number and rang off. I thought that was that, when the phone rang. Mrs Kimba told me to wait by the phone: she had left a message for Dick to contact me.

I waited and waited. After a couple of hours there was a gentle knock on my hotel room door. I opened the door and there stood Dick Kimba. Well, who else could it have been? "G'day. Paul Bura? My name is Dick Kimba, I hear you are looking for me." Hiding behind his legs was the prettiest little girl I had ever seen. This was Dick's little daughter, whose name I'm ashamed to say I have forgotten. I made Dick a cup of tea and we rapped for about an hour. "You got a couple of hours to spare, Paul?" said Dick. I told him that I had exactly three days before I had to get back to Adelaide. "Great, I'd like to show you around Alice, take you to see some of the sacred sites that are still standing. Can you get in a jeep okay?" I was off and flying! This was more than I dared dream!

Dick was a gentle, quiet, bearded man in his mid-forties. He can best be described as the David Bellamy of Aboriginal culture. We talked about Aborigine 'Dream Time', which, roughly translated, means 'eternal', having no beginning and no end.

Dick took me to two sacred sites. The first was a place with just a few bricks where once the house of a white man judge lived. The Aborigines told Dick that the judge did not build the house there for nothing. He was guided to do so, even though he was not aware of it. The judge was a fair man. Perhaps this sacred site inspired his attitude toward the Aborigines. (If I'd had my dowsing rod with me I would have checked out as to whether there was an energy line running through this site, and I'd bet a pound to a dollar there would have been, and a powerful one at that!)

Then I was shown a sacred tree of the 'caterpillar Dream Time'. Here, Dick told me the white man will be shown a tree, cave or wall painting, and be impressed. But the Aborigine will be more interested in a few small stones outside the cave, or sacred place, whose significance only he understands because of the enormous power in nature that floods the land giving the Aborigine signs and indications as to how he should conduct himself and his life. Most white men do not understand this.

Sometimes the white man will ask the Aborigine if he can build a road in a certain place. If the Aborigine says "Yes, it is not sacred," they go ahead. Then, suddenly a piece of rock is unearthed with a design on it. The Aborigines will get very excited in their discussion and tell the white man that this is sacred, that they had forgotten it was there; that it represented something that was in union with another sacred site (an energy line link-up?). The white man doesn't believe the Aborigines and thinks they're being bloody-minded. But Dick says they aren't. They have just lost the knowledge of the place - it is as simple as that!

Until 20 years ago the Aborigines had no rights. Now things are better. Dick told me that Alice means nothing to the Aborigines. Yes, they use its facilities, but they do not know it as a town, only a place with buildings, buildings put there by the white man. None of the town means anything to them; as far as they are concerned Alice does not really exist. The buildings might just as well not be there. The essence of the Aborigine would appear to be that the land is the land - if the white man chooses to be there, that's his choice, but they also choose to be there.

I was introduced to Australia's number one artist: Clifford-Possum (his totem) Jabaljari. He is of the Papunya tribe. His wife's totem is 'Rain'. His grandfather has another totem. After two generations of marrying and mixing, a cycle is formed until each again retains his original totem. Like the Red Indian, they identify with this the supreme consciousness of, say, the dingo as being fierce, who throws up the dirt as he walks, his teeth and jaw very strong. A man will identify with this creature in spirit and hand that strength on down through the generations.

When in the outback, these people, when walking toward a certain point, sing their joy as they get closer, stop and discuss it, then move on again, singing. Dick said what a privilege it was that they accepted and trusted him, and how wonderful it was to hear them sing like that. The whole land sings to them; every rock, bird, animal, tree, is part of Dream Time (or *Alcheringa,* as the Aborigines call it) and speaks to them. Unlike the Red Indian, no pioneer took the time to sit and translate. The difference between the Red Indian and the Aborigine is that they do not have the poetic language of the Indian. Nor is their grasp of the white man's language anything near as good. This is a great barrier. Yet their acknowledgement of the Earth as mother and all her creatures is the same.

An Aborigine does not become a man until he is initiated with ceremony and circumcision. Even if he is 60 years old, if not initiated he is still regarded as a boy. Even the white band around the head means nothing unless he undergoes ceremony. Part of this ceremony includes not sleeping for three days. A pole, representing, say, the caterpillar Dream Time, is placed in the ground. When they wake, the pole will have disappeared into the ground – but this is an illusion perpetrated by the elders, who remove the pole and cover the earth, leaving no sign that it was ever there. Like Santa Claus not being real, but only one's parents dressing up, they believe that the pole disappears. This gives power and respect to the elders. Later, the initiates learn the truth, but at that time they accept the pole's disappearance.

A small incident: some young Aborigines got hold of a cassette recorder and recorded a magic song. Then they got drunk and played it back within earshot of the women. The women are not usually allowed to hear it. When the elders heard of this the young men were severely punished. Dick Kimba told me many things like this; my only regret is that I didn't have a cassette recorder myself, because I missed so much of what he told me.

During our time together, incidents occurred that I could not explain. Firstly, Dick Kimba lived *just around the corner* from the Larrapinta Lodge where I was staying. Secondly, on awakening the next morning after my day out with Dick, I found a small stone in my bed; its shape looked somewhat like South America, whatever that means! I remembered that Dick had taken me up on a hill (I think it was a kind of memorial) overlooking Alice Springs. He was showing me parts of the landscape that were sacred to the Aborigines.

It was quite windy and I had just asked him whether he had knowledge of Aborigine magic. Dick would not be drawn on the subject (darn it!). Suddenly, what seemed like a small stone or large piece of grit hit the seat between us. For a split second Dick looked down on the sound it made, as indeed I did. But that was it, and I then forgot about it. Where did this stone in my bed come from? If the wind had blown a small stone, then it would have blown many small stones, as the ground was covered in them. I distinctly remember feeling a warmth between Dick and myself at about the time the stone struck, a tremor of power.

Dick told me that even a small stone means much more to an Aborigine than perhaps an ancient wall painting by one of

In Australia, Peter Browne, artist and cartoonist, inspects the 'Ju Ju' stick with a certain amount of caution: hence the cigarette!

his ancestors. I kept the stone!

During our trek around Australia, we had met up with the well-known Australian poet and advocate for Aborigine rights, Kath Walker, who lived on Stradbroke Island just off the coast of Brisbane. Together again, John Webster and I had taken the ferry over to the island and I phoned Kath Walker from the kiosk next to the post office. She said to ask directions at the chemist as, it seemed, almost everyone knew her.

We took the dirt track up through a small wood called Moongalba. The white missionaries misnamed it 'Myora'. We parked the Combie outside a corrugated shack. Outside was a wooden bench and a couple of light metal chairs. Suddenly, there she was, striding nimbly towards us, a slight, brown lady in her mid to late 60s. She shook hands with John. "Are you the poet?" she asked. "No, I'm the journalist," he said, "he's the poet," indicating me. She shook my hand and made us sit down. "What do you want to know?" She asked us quite directly, but with friendship in her voice and eyes. "I want to know about the Aborigines. I want to know of their customs, of their inner mystical life." "Ah!" she said, brightening up, "then ask away".

She told us that her totem animal was the carpet snake, which was colourfully carved into one of the trees. Her tribe was the Noo-Nuccle. Apart from being a poet, artist and lecturer on Aborigine culture (she toured the USA, Russia and China, all at the expense of each country), she had taught in excess of 26,000 children from her own Aboriginal folk to white kids from right here in Moongalba. The name Moongalba was the name of the wise man of the Noo-Nuccle tribe who had a special place on Stradbroke Island where he would meditate and try to solve the problems of his people. When the white man came to Stradbroke Island in the form of missionaries, they told the Noo-Nuccle that they must change their heathen ways. The Noo-Nuccle decided to stay in Moongalba which means 'Sitting Down Place'.

Kath's bird totem was the 'Book-Book Owl'. She told us that when a white owl with red eyes appears outside her home it will be time for her to die. "Not yet, though," she said, "I have more to do." She and her tribe believed in reincarnation. "This is my fifth cycle and there could be two more, making seven. I was told that next time I may come back as a carpet snake. I quite like that. No worries."

John asked her about the story he had been told by a white social worker who worked in the Northern Territory with the Aborigines. This social worker told John that the white man still went out and shot black men for sport. Kath nodded her head. "It does not surprise me." She then proceeded to tell us a horrific tale of the severed head of an Aborigine woman aged about 25 years - this was in 1976 - that was sent to Kath after a phone call. Kath made me promise not to repeat the story. Kath Walker died in 1994, one of the only female elders of her tribe: a great honour. Somehow, I believe Kath will forgive me if I tell the tale today as I remember her telling it to John and myself outside her humble corrugated home at Moongalba on Stradbroke Island in 1987:

"I received a telephone call from a friend asking me whether I would like to have the severed head of a young female Aborigine. I asked her what the hell she was talking about. She told me that she was serving drinks in a bar in Brissie when in came this Canadian carrying a brown paper parcel tied with string. He put the parcel down on the stool next to him and ordered a drink. Many drinks later, this Canadian started talking about a black prostitute he had met and subsequently killed. He winked and said that he had her head in the parcel! After a couple more drinks, he passed out. My friend took the parcel home and opened it. It was indeed a severed head. She put it in the fridge and phoned me. I told her to bring it over as soon as she could. When it arrived, I dug a hole in my back garden and covered it over. I put thirteen rings of small stones around the hole and waited. "What for?" asked John. "I had to wait for the Butcher birds to come! I waited ten days, then one morning I could hear the Butcher birds making a racket. I went to the grave and there the rings of stones had been disturbed. It was what I had been waiting for. The soul of that young Aborigine was now released and would go into Dream Time."

Kath Walker and I swapped books, her poems for mine. I would have liked to have known her better, but time was short. We had to leave. I wonder whether, prior to her passing into Dream Time, a red-eyed, white owl winked at her?

CHAPTER 20

On my return to England from Oz, I was asked by the new owners of *Manna* (our old health store) whether I would consider working part-time for them again. I agreed. It was during this time that I was approached by Channel 4 to see if I was interested in being a reporter for a TV programme called *Same Difference*, a series that reflected the needs and plight of the disabled. The producer was Martin Davison and the chief presenter was Peter White, the blind writer and broadcaster (I once gave him a Braille photograph of a naked lady. I'm not sure whether he saw the joke). I auditioned and was accepted. Mind you, the title 'reporter' was a joke. All I did was read the words! Later, though, I did do 'pieces to camera' (or 'piss on the camera' as we called it).

Eventually, I had to interview Bill Podmore, the then producer of *Coronation Street*, with opening shots of me coming out of the house next to the corner shop and doing my 'piece to the camera' as I walked down that famous street, trying hard not to fall over. Now comes a confession. *I stole the loo chain from the toilet in the Rovers Return* as a memento! I have a feeling that I wasn't the only one to have done so 'cos the one I swiped was a 'spare'. It was lying on the window-sill and I just could not resist it.

When we did internal scenes with Bill Podmore in 'The Rovers' (there are two *Rovers Returns* - the external one you see where folk are going IN, and the internal one where you see people supping ale), I had the producer and his assistant standing behind me feeding me the bloody questions! Poor old Bill must have thought me a real prat. Still, it looked okay on the screen, which is what really matters.

By this time my family were getting restless. My mother had wanted to move from Herne Bay for a long time and my sister Josie, who had just gone through a nasty divorce which had at last been settled with a little money, also wanted out. We decided to move to West Sussex to be near my younger sister Mellie, who lived in Worthing with her husband, Frank, and two boys.

On the Coronation Street set when I was sent to interview the then Producer, Bill Podmore. I nicked the loo chain!

We put the house in Bullers Avenue on the market and within a few months had sold it. We moved to Lancing in 1988, just down the road from Worthing. Within the space of a few weeks I had found a shop with living accommodation, ideal for another health store (Manna two) where Josie could live. I lived just around the corner with mother. (Later, I converted the upstairs loft into separate living accommodation for myself, all paid for by my work with Channel 4.)

Josie and I pooled our money with my mother and within a month of completion the shop was stocked and open. The first four years were fine, but then the recession began to bite. Business began to level out and then to drop. Unemployment was very high and businesses of all descriptions were going down the tubes.

However, during that time I fell deeply and disastrously in love. 1989 was one of the most painful of experiences, an obsessional love that left me bruised and bleeding. In order to take my mind off of the focus of my love, I started to brush-up on my dowsing skills.

My very dear friend, Malcolm Ing, a fine psychic and painter (the man who vanished, you will remember) once told me that we all lived in a hologram. It wasn't until I started more advanced dowsing that I understood what he actually meant. Let me explain: The art of dowsing is, as many of you no doubt know, more than just the ability to find water with a forked hazel twig. In fact, you can dowse for ANYTHING. What fascinated me more than anything else was the ability to 'bring the world into my own living room' merely by map dowsing. So how does 'living in a hologram' come into this?

Okay; a hologram is a three-dimensional image projected by lasers. The image projected is captured on a holographic glass plate through which the lasers are played. If one were to break the plate in two, in one half of the plate the same three-dimensional image will appear. If you were to then break that half into quarters, you would *still* have the full image, and so on. Now, with map dowsing – the ability to find earth energy lines and places of power, not to mention water and minerals – you can bring the place that you wish to dowse right into your living-room! For example, suppose I wanted to find an old Celtic temple that rumour has it used to be in a certain area. Using an Ordnance Survey map, I would grid off the area indicated with a pencil and, using a pendulum and a pointer, would carefully scan the area indicated until I got a positive reaction - in my case a clockwise rotation of my pendulum. I would then grid off *that* area and start the procedure all over again until I found the precise point as to where the supposed temple once stood (not that I personally could physically trudge through fields to find what was left of the temple, but I, of course, always know someone who can!).

Now can you see what I mean by 'living in a hologram'? You can, by an act of visualisation, bring, for instance, the dowsable image of an ancient standing stone, hundreds of miles away, into your front room and dowse the energies around it. Then, when you have the time and inclination, you can drive those hundreds of miles away and prove your findings!

Why would I wish to bring such a large object into my house? Standing stones that are part of the earth energy grid invariably have seven bands of energy running up them that correspond with the seven chakric points of the human body – (in fact there are eight, but more of that later). These chakric points are easily dowsed. Places of power that are part of the earth grid system consist of churches (usually pre-reformation), standing stones like those of Avebury and Stonehenge, tumuli, ancient ponds, temple sites, and even modern monoliths and architecture, where the creative, though sometimes destructive powers of Mankind are used.

This earth grid is likened to the 'meridian' lines that the Chinese use when applying their acupuncture needles: if the energy in the body is blocked, causing various ills, then a needle carefully and accurately placed can unblock the said energy. It is the same with the earth energy grid. If a house is giving off bad vibrations causing unexplainable illness to its occupants, invariably you will find that an earth energy line that has been contaminated is running through the house. An experienced dowser will be able to transmute that energy into healing energy! Fascinating, huh?

Talking of healing energy, I must tell you about the most bizarre healing session that I have EVER witnessed. This was done in 1992. My mother suffers from nasal problems and has done so all her life. She always has a handkerchief close to hand and is constantly blowing her nose trying to clear it. She'd had the usual 'clearance job' done by the local hospital, but when she tried to tell them they were washing out the wrong side she was told: "Don't be silly, we know what we're doing" (silly woman). A pity they didn't read the notes!

So when a customer came into our health food Store in Lancing, and told me that she had just undergone psychic surgery on her back which was completely successful, that this surgeon was a German field-doctor in the First World War and was using the body of a carpenter (no, not that carpenter), I pricked up my ears. On further questioning, this lady had gone with her friend to see this doctor, and accompanied her into the surgery. I can't remember what she had done, but on the way out the German doctor said suddenly: "You hev za problem wiz you beck." "Yes, I do," said my customer, "in fact I have done so for the last 20 years. I have to lie down on the floor in order to sleep. Apparently there is nothing physically wrong with me." "I can cure you," said the German doctor.

With her permission he lay her on her tummy, and with her friend as a witness he made a small incision with a scalpel at the base of her spine. Then, using a teaspoon he scraped it and closed the wound leaving a small red line, which disappeared within a few days. She no longer had a problem and she could now use a normal bed. I took the name and telephone number of the doctor and made an appointment for my mother.

The day arrived and I took her on the two hour journey to the surgery. When we arrived there was a queue of people; that was before you registered and paid the fee. The waiting room was a heaving mass of humanity. There was a book with newspaper cuttings from all the people who had been helped or cured by this man. Hundreds of them.

At last, our time came. My mother, who by now was very nervous, asked whether I could come too (you couldn't keep me out of there. I wanted to see EVERYTHING). The doctor nodded his approval and was surprised when it was my *mother* who was to be his patient and not me. I guess when a bloke, leaning on his mother's shoulder, limping profusely and carrying a stick, staggers in... well what conclusion would you come to?

"Vood you mine getting on za couch?" Mother nodded and did so. "Vood you mine if I feelink your tummy?" Mother nodded again, holding my hand as he did so. "Hmmm," he said, rubbing alcohol on mother's stomach, picking up a scalpel, "I sink ve make und cut... here!" With that, he sliced a four inch gash in my mother's tummy and with a pair of surgical tweezers rummaged around until he apparently *felt* something. At this point, the grip from my mother's hands felt like a pair of pliers! She didn't feel any pain (I damn well did!), only extremely uncomfortable from Herr Doctor's rummaging. And there's me, not two feet away, witnessing the whole procedure. The doctor suddenly found what he was looking, or feeling for, pulled 'it' out and flicked it into a bin. The wound by now was a little bloody. He wiped it clean and the wound disappeared except for a little red line.

"What was this to do with her nasal passages?" I thought. Out in the hall he put his arm around my mother's shoulder and said: "You should rest for a couple of ze days. You have just had ze operation. Come and see me in a couple of za weeks, Yar? My mother nodded and duly made the appointment. The next time we saw the Herr Doctor, all he did was the laying on of hands. My mother said to him "Why did you operate on my stomach when I specifically said that it was my nasal passages that needed attending to?" The Herr Doctor remained silent. Again he said to make a further appointment.

This time he *really* meant business. Before you could say 'sauerkraut' he was at it again! He made a tiny incision under my mother's left eye with the scalpel. He reeled back slightly. Apparently, the sinus passages that run under the eyes were blocked and smelly. Then, picking up a hammer and what I can only describe as a surgical chisel, he began to whack the cheek-bone just under her eye. I'm sitting there not three feet away! Whack! Whack! Whack! Whack! At one point, he said to his wife (the carpenter's wife) to "hold za head still." After four or five more whacks he put down his hammer and chisel, closed the wound with a touch of his hand and that was it! I couldn't believe what I had just witnessed, I just could not believe it!

On the way out he said: "Vot is za metter viz you?" "Polio," I said. "It is karmic," he said, "I can do nothing for you. I am sorry." I already knew it, of course. But I'd come for my mother's benefit and not my own.

My mother's condition since? It's exactly the same as it was. Maybe it too was karmic... but why couldn't he have said so?

CHAPTER 21

At the end of 1992, John Cole, a teacher at Lancing College (one of its old boys was Tim Rice of *Evita* and *Jesus Christ Superstar* fame) started coming into the shop. We got talking and he happened to mention crop circles, the intricate swirled shapes which appear in fields each summer! Crop circles interested me. I couldn't explain why, but one thing I knew; they were not all man-made hoaxes. John was the treasurer for CCCS Sussex (the then local branch of the Centre for Crop Circle Studies, later to become known as Southern Circular Research) and suggested that I come along to a meeting. After a couple of false starts, I eventually went along. My interest in dowsing caught the attention of Andy Thomas, the editor of SC (or *Sussex Circular*), their periodic journal on the crop circle phenomenon. "Why don't you give a talk and a demonstration on dowsing?" he said. So I did.

What I didn't know was that the bastard had already got an Ordnance Survey map ready for me to dowse possible crop circles: a test to see whether I was able to find an area where a circle had already appeared and, indeed, where one *might* appear. I was really put on the spot. My results turned out to be a bit naff. I was a newcomer so had no idea where the local crop circles had appeared, though I was close! After that, Andy and I became very good friends. He was fascinated by the mystical side of life and when I mentioned the idea of doing a 'sitting' with a group of people with the idea of trying to contact the Earth Spirit, he readily agreed. This was my first introduction to an entity called 'Joeb'. (The fuller story of all this is told in the book *Quest For Contact*, which I later wrote with Andy.)

On the 13th of August 1992 at around eight o'clock in the evening, a group of about 10 people, including Andy Thomas, my friends Mark and Jason Porthouse and their mother Sylvia, and a few others sat around our very large oak table in the downstairs dining room. The table was festooned with corn taken from various 'genuine' (as far as we could tell) crop circles, plus pictures of a formation which had appeared near my home that year and other assorted designs from years past, carefully reproduced on paper. Incense burned and candles flickered. A lousy old cassette recorder waited to record God knows what! The evening howled with wind and rain hurled itself against the windows. It was a full Moon.

None of us had any idea what to expect, including myself. We had gathered to try and contact the Earth Spirit, Gaia (soon to be called Ayesha), or SOMETHING that might help us in our quest to contact the Circle Makers, whoever and whatever they were.

I sat at the head of the table and conducted the ceremony. I gave the Invocation, under God, to the Earth Spirit and all those who were associated with Her. Then I sat back and waited in meditation. After a few minutes, my breathing began to deepen, energy played around my head and shoulders and down my arms. My throat began to contract, my facial muscles tightened and I knew that someone wanted to communicate. After a few seconds, a terrible urge to speak came upon me. I let it happen! The entity was male and spoke in very dramatic tones concerning forthcoming Earth changes and how the Earth Mother was in pain and that he was Her servant.

He spoke not of crop circles, but of the changes to our southern coastline, while emphasising that warnings would be given. He spoke of his love for the Earth Mother whom he loved and adored. Then he was gone. I came out of it fairly easily, not having channelled for quite some time. Everybody was a little shocked and a little shaken, but intrigued nonetheless. There really wasn't much to say other than: "Does anyone want to do this again?" There was a resounding "Yes!"

Something of this reminded me of a similar 'sitting' that I had held in Herne Bay a few years back with my very good friends Malcolm Murdock - the visionary of the stones on Salisbury Plain - Malcolm Ing and his wife Ros. We had been sitting for quite a few months, mainly in meditative mode, though visions were also seen from time to time. On this occasion, 15th December 1986 - coincidentally, also a full Moon - we had been told by psychic means that an entity would be speaking with us and to be prepared.

I hoped that it would not be me who would be chosen to be the mouthpiece. It was always me and I thought it was about time some other bugger had a go! I truly wanted out of this one. But no, the entity then also spoke of vast Earth changes with possibly millions dying. Malcolm Ing thought it was total balls, but I had had visions of Earth disasters for years (an overactive and dramatic imagination?), somehow 'knowing' of the impending changes, so it came as no surprise to me.

From that later stormy night on the 13th of August 1992, we started weekly sittings. The entity that spoke to us, I now realise, was the same entity that communicated in 1986. The entity who we all came to know, respect and love was a spiritual teacher called 'Joeb' (pronounced *Jobe*). "*Not THE Job of the first book of the Bible, but Joeb, spelled J.O.E.B.*" He was a Burmese Buddhist priest in his last life, but always claimed that he was not a very good Buddhist and was more of a spiritual counsellor to the small village Myebon in Burma. He lived in a cave high above the village. The cave was part of a cliff that backed onto the sea.

Joeb encouraged all those sitting to ask him questions and he would answer the best way he could. This question and answer system was Joeb's method of teaching. He taught us his method of Earth Healing by the use of crystals and visualisation. With Earth changes already taking place, this method was designed to ease the Earth Mother gently into a higher frequency. Of course, the idea of the Earth ascending into a higher vibration is not new, but that time was now! And she could do with all the help she could get! Now is the time that has been foreseen for so long by so many visionaries. The negative forces *know* that the Earth will change and they *know* that they will soon be out of a job, no longer in control of the planet. They are being squeezed out, though to look at this planet at the moment you would hardly think so. Joeb says it will get worse before it gets better and the opposition will pull out every stop in order to hold on to the Earth they have dominated since before Atlantis.

Joeb went to great pains to prove to us who he was. He couldn't prove to us that he was once a Buddhist priest (16th Century), but he *could* prove to us his life BEFORE that in England when he was a trainee 'Priest of the Stones'. Joeb told me that he once lived in what is now Sudbury at the end of the 1st Century and the beginning of the 2nd Century AD. Joeb urged me to get a road map and look up Sudbury. Unfortunately there are THREE Sudburys in England. That proved not to be a problem. I let Joeb control me whilst I looked through the various Sudburys. When I got to Sudbury in Suffolk, I felt a huge surge of energy. This was the one!

Next, I had to get an Ordnance Survey map of Suffolk. Joeb told me, or rather I received impressions, that his village was near water, but that the spot to map-dowse was where his old stone circle once stood! Using the grid-system, I map-dowsed the area and pinpointed a certain spot that, yes, was right on a riverbank, the river Stour. By now, our little group of sitters were beginning to swell in number and amongst that number was a master dowser, David Russell. David had had years of experience and counts amongst his dowsing friends Colin Bloy and the late Michael Bentine. I asked David to check my findings. He took his pendulum and went to work. "Yes," he said after a while, "I agree with your findings, but you're not quite accurate. It should be there!" David pointed to where I had made my mark and moved his pointer one sixteenth of an inch to the right! Well, that was good enough for me.

A few months later, David Russell, Andy Thomas, Quenton Cole (my nephew) and I set off for Sudbury in Suffolk. After a couple of hours, on the outskirts of Sudbury, we stopped for lunch where David and I decided to map-dowse for the actual village where Joeb once lived. We found it, both our pendulums whirling in tandem as we hit the spot on the map.

The place nearest to Joeb's supposed circle was a place called 'Valley Walk' near the village of Borley. (Borley is the site of the famous Borley

Rectory: the most haunted house in England. Joeb told us that during his day it was merely a 'gateway between worlds,' a temple where entities could come and go, but it was abused and all hell broke loose. Borley Rectory was burned down many years ago.)

The Downs Walk meanders its way past the bottom of Borley Hall's driveway, then across country. I parked the car, whilst the others gathered their dowsing rods and maps ready for the walk. I expected a long wait in the car. Something that I had got used to. Suddenly Quenton came bounding back along the path. "You can drive RIGHT there!" he said. He slid into the passenger-seat and we were off! As we drove along, Andy and David loomed into view. David had already picked up the direction, and within only a few minutes the dowsing rods were pointing at a ploughed field; where, incidentally, I could park, facing the area where we believed Joeb's stones once stood.

Quenton got there first, following the far perimeter of the field. I could see him clearly waiting for David and Andy to catch up. Little did I or Quenton know that he was standing almost exactly in the middle of where once were Joeb's stones! I tuned in and felt a wave of excitement. Joeb told me that this was the place.

After about half an hour they returned to the car. "The outer circle is 30 meters wide," said David, wiping the mud from his boots. "The inner circle is about 10 meters, but I couldn't get near the centre because there's a ditch." (Joeb had told us the outer circle had energy running anti-clockwise, the inner circle the energy ran clockwise. In the centre of the two stone circles were a group of smaller stones grouped in a horseshoe shape; this was known as 'The Seat of Power'.) Later, we map-dowsed the site and found the outer circle had nine stones, the inner circle eight stones, and the Seat of Power five stones.

We then decided to find the site of Joeb's village. He had told us that his people were known as the people of 'Oric'. We found the site only a few miles away. Without permission from the farmer, we decided not to get too close to the site of the village, but the site of the graveyard (now a ploughed field) was, according to David, whose knowledge of Celtic life is considerable, very typical of a Celtic graveyard: on a slope near water, the field curving down to the river below.

We had brought posies of flowers as a gift to the 'Guardian' of the circle site, and also for the Earth Goddess herself. We had only one posy left. We intended to dowse for Joeb's grave and place the flowers on top of it as a gesture of respect! In the car Joeb spoke: "I appreciate the gesture, my friends, but it was a long time ago. The bones of that body are long gone. But I appreciate the thought. You have done well today. Now you have some proof of my existence, and I thank you all for your work."

CHAPTER 22

*T*his is an edited transcript of an interview with Joeb conducted by Michael Green RIBA, FSA, the then Chairman, now President, of the Centre for Crop Circle Studies, whose experience in occult and archaeological matters is well-respected. He had asked me whether Joeb would mind such an interview; from the following I think that you will see that he did not.

JOEB TO CCCS SUSSEX AND MICHAEL GREEN
CHANNELLED THROUGH PAUL BURA 21.9.93

PREAMBLE

M: Heavenly Father/Earth Mother, we ask for your guidance this afternoon to remember what has been in the past.

J: Good afternoon to you Mr Green.

M: Good afternoon, Joeb.

J: I take it you are well.

M: I am well and pleased to be here with you. Joeb, I have come this afternoon not specifically to talk about crop formations, although there may be possibly one or two little things at the end of our session I would be grateful for your views on. It is primarily to think back, to try and remember your incarnation as a priest in this country a long time ago, to open the akashic record, to try to remember as far back as you can.... I am not here to catch you out. I am happy to accept what you can remember of the conditions, the rites, the teaching that you had in those far off days. It is of value to me - even small things may be of value to me - so this is what I would like to do.

JOEB THE PRIEST

J: I have already given information to this man (Paul Bura) and I have given him visions as best I can of my life amongst the stones. As you know, I was not exactly a priest. I was more of an underling and I described myself as a kind of curate. I have also described to you my vision when I was a young boy. My father was the chief of this tribe, the people of Oric (*NOTE 1*). Through a mistake of the channelling of this man (Paul) -sometimes it is difficult to give names through him – he was saying Eric, which caused great laughter among the people in this group! But it was the people of Oric of which my father was the chief. Indeed he was a great father to me, but I remember even as a child I had done this work before in a past life, and I did not really wish to become a priest, but my father was most insistent that I do this. So he dragged me kicking and screaming to the priests, wearing my white robe with gold, and he presented me to them. And I was accepted. Mind you, it was difficult for them to refuse – after all my father was the chief. But the head priest was a very powerful man in his own right.

TRIBAL RITES OF PASSAGE: PUBERTY

M: You must, presumably, as a child have had rites of passage, initiations into adult life. Can you remember any of these at all?

J: Yes, there were certain rites. Yes, indeed there were initiations. The priests ruled our lives. But it was good and beautiful, although we feared them and respected them at the same time. There were rites amongst the stones as young men, as youths. This would happen at five years old, when we would be taken to the stones for initiations. Normally, this would involve taking fruit and grains and would be at a certain time of year, and these would be offered to the priests who would, in turn, offer them to the Earth Mother, whom you know now we called 'Ayesha' (*NOTE 2*). This was a great moment for all of us. The whole of the tribe, men, women and children would come. It was at the age of 10 that I was first introduced to the priests. But there was no sacrifice of any kind.

M: Did you have to go apart for a while, on your own, as it were.

J: Yes, indeed.

M: Where did you go? Did you sit out in the stones or did you go somewhere else?

J: No, we were told to go out into the wild and sit and meditate for a couple of days. We were given a minimum of food, perhaps, fruit and bread and water. The idea was that it would stimulate us into a receptive and meditative state, as you would call it today.

M: Did you do anything while you were sitting meditating? Can you remember?

J: We were told to offer ourselves to Ayesha, and we would sit there amongst ourselves. We would sit around a fire. We were instructed to do nothing but sit this way and meditate.

PRIESTLY TRAINING

M: But the rites and the teaching for the children who were going to become priests or shamans would have been rather more intensive?

J: Yes, oh very...

M: How long was your training, can you remember?

J: My training from the age of 10 was five years. We were very much dogsbodies.

M: Can you remember the main areas of work that you had to do?

J: There was much heavy work, practical work. We would have to do practical work. When I say this, I mean that there were special foods that had to be prepared for certain ceremonies. There would be the looking after of all the livestock, because there were certain animals that were set aside for the priests and others and for my father and heads of the tribe, and then other animals were also set aside for the people. We raised pigs. We would also grow wheat and corn.

STATUS OF THE PRIESTHOOD

M: Did the priests live in the village or were they in a separate part of the settlement?

J: They were part of us. But they also had what you would call today a 'priest hole' made of wood and stones which was nearer to the stones. They would only go there prior to the big ceremony at the stones. They would go there to prepare.

M: This 'priest hole' was a sort of men's lodge?

J: Yes, indeed so.

TEACHING OF THE PRIESTHOOD

M: One obviously knows a little about the rites, but the main area which I am interested in is, of course, the teaching which you had over many years. It is going to be difficult to give anything in detail, but perhaps you can give the main areas of teaching, if you can...

J: All our lives were dominated by Ayesha and the ideal of the female principle. We revered females, it was very necessary for them to be revered. We appreciated that the Earth was female and therefore it was a privilege for us to be on her surface, as it is indeed today. She provided us with everything – everything – and therefore it is for us to tune in and appreciate the great glory of the mother Earth – Ayesha. There was much to do in terms of ceremony. The whole of my young life was taken up with hard work, and the teaching work would become an extension of this. It was handed down, of course, from the priest, and he would teach us that they came from a long, long way away. I believe now, though I did not know then, that it was Egypt (*NOTE 3*) they initially came from, but many hundreds of years before.

M: You were presumably part of the Trinovantes or the tribe of the Iceni.

INITIATION RITES OF THE PRIESTHOOD

M: The tribal children were taught in the village rather than the men's lodge?

J: No, they would only go out to the sacred places outside the stones when they were a certain age. This was a very sacred ground; we would be taken out of the village for an initiation ceremony to these places – a great ceremony. But we were afraid because we knew of the great power. Not only of the priest, but also of the stones.

M: The stone circle doesn't survive any longer in that area?

J: No.

M: Can you remember any details of the layout of the circle,

how it was used?

J: Yes, I can.

M: The site, the circle, was it just a simple circle of stones?

J: No, it was a circle within a circle. There was a large outer circle, it was a henge, I think you call it. Around the outside of the circle the energy was flowing anti-clockwise. In the case of the inner circle, which was a complete circle, the energy flowed clockwise. In the middle of this circle was a horseshoe shape, and this was called the 'Seat of Power', a group of stones in a horseshoe shape. It is through this that energy lines would go. More than two I believe, maybe three. But the main energy line was where the head priests, after much ceremony, would have all the villagers (what you would call today) circle dancing around the stones. You would have one area of people with their own personal energy and they would be singing to Ayesha and chanting, and they would dance around the circle, the outer circle in alignment with the anti-clockwise movement. The other line of people would be in the second circle, the inner circle, and they would go in a clockwise direction. This used to bring out the energy. Although the energy was there already, this brought it up to a fantastic crescendo and the stones would store this energy until a point of saturation had been reached. At this point, the priest who would be sitting in the Seat of Power, would disappear.

M: Disappear?!

J: Yes, indeed, he would disappear down the line of energy and would appear at another stone site many, many, sometimes hundreds of miles away. He would then be able to pick up information. It was a mode of travel, and he would be able to also return in this way.

M: Did he return during the same rite?

J: Yes, indeed, and come back with many stories (*NOTE 5*). Sometimes he would travel to a similar circle, to people who were in allegiance with us, and sometimes he would travel to other dimensions.

THE RITUAL OF THE RINGS OF POWER

M: The people who formed the Rings of Power, was there any particular way in which they danced or held hands?

J: They held hands and they would dance. They would have their hands on each others' shoulders, and they would dance around in rhythm, with the way of the energy. This way first and then the inner circle would go that way.

M: Was there any sort of accompaniment?

J: Yes, indeed, there was a drummer. We had a ceremonial drummer. This was a hard-wood drum. A long, hard-wood drum which was hollowed out of (probably) oak. This was polished very dry and it was off the ground. Sometimes as many as three drummers were on the same log...

This is an edit of a much longer interview, just to give you a flavour of Joeb's life then.

NOTES (by Michael Green)

1)   *Oric.*   In an earlier transmission in 1993, Joeb described his father's name in the incarnation in question as being 'Erik'. Since he had also identified the place (Sudbury in Suffolk) and the date, early second century AD, this caused, even for the non-expert, some difficulty. However, in this channeling he corrected the name to Oric, and there is a possibility that it was also a clan name. Names are important since their etymology is the best possible indicator for the ethnic origins of a tribal group.

'Eric' and 'Oric', are perfectly respectable northern European names of the migration period. Oric is cognitive with *Ori*, which appears in the *Edda* of the medieval, Icelandic chronicler Snorri Sturluson as one of the stone dwarfs (in our terms, an Earth Deva) in *Gylfaginning* 14-15. Both Uric and Aesir (see note 2) indicate that Joeb's clan or 'sept' had northern European connections.

2)   *Aesir.*   This name of the Earth Goddess, pronounced by Joeb 'Ayesha' in this communication, would appear to be totally unrelated to any known proper name for the Earth Goddess in the Celtic World. However, the Northmen of the Migration Age called the race of their gods *Aesir* from a singular form ass meaning 'deity'. The process by which the personal name of a god became the generative title of a group of secondary deities or Devas under the Being's *aegis* is well known from the Celtic

tradition. In the *Lebor Gabala Erenn* (the 'book of the taking of Ireland'), which is a medieval reduction of prehistoric traditions regarding the origin of the Irish people, the seventh and last group to arrive were the Tuatha de Dadaan. This company, which comprised the principal deities of the Celto-Irish pantheon, had as its collective name the title of the Earth Goddess Dana, called in other contexts Dana or Annan. The parallel with Aesir, which comprised the principal gods of the Scandinavian world, is significant.

3) *Egypt.* Establishing a respectable lineage (in folk terms) was a central element in traditional teaching. The *Lebor Gabala Erenn* (see note 2) has identical Celtic tradition as regards Egypt; "...in the land of Egypt thereafter, was born Gaedel our father" (sect.1.58).

4) *The Megalithic Sanctuary.* The details concerning the sacred structure and its use are of extraordinary interest. It brings together various elements: the geodetic and astronomical alignment; the function of ritual, song and dance deliberately used as a dynamic process for raising the 'etheric power'; and the uses to which the power was put. No Stonehenge-like monuments have ever been recorded this far east in England, and if they ever existed they must have been rarer than those recorded in the north and west. However, it is possible that the glacial erratics from the Boulder Clay could have been used for constructional purposes. The monument, as described by Joeb, is unusually complex (even of its type) with its double ring and central 'cove', as archaeologists term this particular feature. The nearest surviving examples are to be found in the Derbyshire group, and in particular at Arbor Low which has a 'cove' and continued as a focus of local worship into the Bronze Age (Aubrey Burl, *Stone Circles of the British Isles*). In the area there is another 'Sudbury."

5) *Spirit Travel.* Although ostensibly bizarre, indeed unbelievable in any conventional sense, such disappearances are well attested to in the records of psychical research and, indeed, folklore. King Bladud, eponymous cultural hero and shaman, was killed when his powers failed as he was approaching Stonehenge on a spirit flight (*Chronicle of John Hardynge 1543*). Spirit Travel, and the psychic experiences gained thereby, was a central feature of shamanic groups in central and northern Asia within living memory (Miscea Eliade, *Shamanism*).

CHAPTER 23

One of the topics that Joeb returns to again and again is his referral to most human beings as being 'Earth addicts'. "You are all addicted to something or other. It might be food, pain, sex, drink, drugs, even love. Of course, I do not mean unconditional love, but love that destroys, love that smothers, love that obsesses. There is nothing at all the matter with food and sex and drink taken in moderation. But what we seek here is 'balance'. The whole world is out of balance. The earth energy grid is out of balance, the world between spirit and matter is out of balance. The Yin and Yang.

Male humans must find the female aspect within and likewise the female must recognise the male. The spirit planes around the Earth are jam-packed with souls waiting to incarnate for all the lessons they have failed to learn in countless lives. And why? Because they are all addicted to Earth. They have not yet learned to let go and therefore go forward to greater planes of existence, places that are so fantastic you cannot even imagine it. You are all asleep! You must wake up and find out who you are, where you have come from and where you are going. NOW is the time to do this."

"This is a special time in Earth history. The Earth Mother, Ayesha, has to ascend to a higher frequency. Most of you here have a job to do and that main job is to wake up! Then you can start the work you have incarnated for this time around. The old religions are crumbling and the source (God) will not encourage another religion to take their place, only a glorious realisation that you are ALL gods in the making, that you have the God-spark within. The whole of the Universe is within you, all that 'is' is within you. You have to realise it. The sooner you do, the sooner My Lady Ayesha can ascend to where she belongs."

A few months after Joeb's appearance, another entity came through during a sitting. This was a Sioux Indian named Grey Wolf. Now I know many of you will think: why are guides and teachers always either Red Indians, Chinese or Egyptian? The simple answer is that they lived so near to nature, certainly in the case of the Red Indian nations. As has already been said concerning the Aboriginals of Australia, these people KNOW the Earth Spirit. I'm still waiting for an enlightened bank manager to manifest! Anyhow, getting back to Grey Wolf, he was a Sioux Medicine man whose job was to teach us to open the third eye (the brow chakra). This he did by visualisation and the use of crystals; crystals he treated as living beings, part of the consciousness of the great Earth Mother.

Grey Wolf will hold a large amethyst crystal and ask us to pour out of our third eye region all the stress, all the hatred, all the emotional baggage that we may have built up during the week, and also the karmic baggage and pain that remains locked in the subconscious. He calls this 'Karmic Clinker.' This helps to clear the third eye and release stress. The pulling and tugging sensation that the sitters feel around this chakric point cannot be denied! "In the old days, when I was training the apprentices in my tribe, I would bang the third eye area with a rock. This was done with ceremony and herbs. Today we are not so barbaric!" he told us.

The next to join 'The Team', as I now call them, was Black Hawk, a Plains Apache. Black Hawk taught us about 'the breath.' How to breathe using colours. As many of you already know, each chakra has a colour: the Base Chakra is red, the Spleen/Sacral Chakra is orange, the Solar Plexus is yellow, the Heart Chakra is green, the Throat Chakra is blue, the Third Eye Chakra is indigo, the Crown Chakra is violet or purple. There are in fact EIGHT main chakras to date. The eighth Chakra is the Cosmic Chakra. This centre is used for communication beyond this solar system. But more of that later.

Black Hawk taught us first of all to ask our Higher Self to give us a colour, a colour that would benefit the individual. Once we had our colour (if anyone found getting their colour difficult, Black Hawk would give them their colour on request) we would breathe in the visualised colour deeply through the nose, then hold the breath for a few seconds and slowly release the breath through the mouth. We would do this seven times. He also taught us to pray for special things using this method. On the inward breath (in this case using white light) we would make our request to the source, on the outward breath we would visualise the result of our request to God, breathing the white light over our vision.

The fourth member of The Team came when I least expected it. I was sitting with the group waiting for Grey Wolf to communicate in his usual manner when I realised that the character coming through was NOT Grey Wolf, but someone else. I asked who it was and was shown a picture of ANOTHER Red Indian. (When Joeb describes a guide or teacher to a sitter and it turns out to be a Red Indian, he always says: "Oh no, ANOTHER Red Indian!"). This entity called himself Red Fox. I let him come through and he told us that he wished (me) to build a medicine wheel which would consist of four wooden poles, four feet high, erected on the exact cardinal points of the compass. On top of each pole we were to put large amethyst crystals the size of my fist. The recipient would sit in the middle facing North, whilst Red Fox (via me) would, with the use of two clear quartz crystals, balance the chakras of the body and assist with healing.

What was I to do? If I built a medicine wheel and it didn't work, I would end up with a lot of psychic egg on my face! I asked the group if they wanted me to go ahead. Of course, there was a positive response. They were as curious as I.

My nephew Quenton built the medicine wheel (which is affectionately known as the 'Zap Machine') and we tried it out. The result was astounding! When the recipient is seated and comfortable Red Fox gently rotates the crystals in his/my hands, pointing at the heart region. After a while a gentle warmth is generated in this area. When this is achieved, he moves up to the Throat Chakra. The warmth in this area is very often accompanied by a pressure on the throat; this indicates to Red fox that the sitter is capable of channelling one way or another. And he's always right. Then, from the throat region up to the Third Eye Chakra. Again, pressure can be felt here, but this does not always signify that the recipient will develop clairvoyance. Then finally up to the Crown Chakra where he releases the energy.

Red Fox also identifies and names guides and teachers associated with the recipient. This is followed by any healing that the person concerned may need, on request.

One of the most startling healings that Red Fox was involved in was for one of our members called Kim. She was an ex-Greenham Common lady and fought very hard for the anti-nuclear cause. However, she believed she had been zapped, as so many were, by microwaves that the Americans bombarded these brave women with. The result was extreme headaches, nausea and noises in the head. No doctor could help. Kim suffered for years with this condition, but after a few sessions in the Zap Machine she was a new woman and became a medium (channeller) and healer herself. (Sadly, Kim is no longer with us.)

The negativity that the amethyst crystals picks up is counted on a one to ten base. Red Fox will say when the crystals need cleansing and one of our members present will perform this simple task of crystal cleansing using a pendulum. This is done by requesting that the universal Self cleanse the crystal. The pendulum simply indicates when the process is complete. It usually takes about 30 seconds.

Each member of The Team has his own personality. Black Hawk has a very deep voice and sounds very much like one would expect a Red Indian to sound like, except he never says 'How!' When you first hear him, one imagines him to put up with no nonsense and to be completely humourless. Not true on any count. In fact the whole Team burst with good humour, none more so than Joeb.

Red Fox is gentle but firm with an exactness about him, which is quite disarming. Grey Wolf sounds like a professor and also possesses a dry wit. They all command respect without even trying. Joeb once said that it was because he was a discarnate being that people listened to him. But he was, in my view, just being modest. There is something about all of them that commands respect and love. I feel privileged to work with them, though I do so on a less regular basis now.

CHAPTER 24

*I*became more and more involved with the crop circle phenomenon. For me, one of the greatest thrills was contacting 'Site Guardians.' "What is a 'Site Guardian?" I hear you say. Through very personal experience, I became aware that every section of the Earth has a Guardian whose job it is to keep the energy lines clear of contamination. Contamination can come in the form of mining operations, where the earth is dug-up for minerals, or from new roads and byways, which play havoc with the earth energy grid. This is not an easy job. When Humankind were aware of the energy grid they paid more respect as to where they mined and built houses and roads. The Chinese with their Feng-Shui, pronounced Fung-Shway, meaning 'wind and water', believe these two forces form the landscape and with their various instruments would never dream of building a road or house, or ANY structure, without having first surveyed using the laws of geomancy.

Guardians come in all shapes and sizes. The ones that I've worked with are human in form, having had, as we have, many earthly incarnations. But there are those who are of the Devic realms, who do their best to keep humans away from places of wild beauty and power. These beings, these Nature Spirits, do not trust us one little bit, and can you blame them? What we have done and what we are continuing to do to the Earth Mother is appalling and they want as little to do with us as possible.

There are other Guardians that are of a rather sinister variety. These are grotesque projections of thought put at various sites to scare the hell out of people, people who might just be getting too near to a ritualistic site of sinister occult power. I am, of course, talking of the Dark Ones. That is not to say that White magicians can't also conjure up these incredibly realistic monsters, complete with sound, to protect their own places of power!

One story worth telling, concerning a bunch of dowsers, occurred at the top of the Iron Age hillfort Cissbury Ring, in West Sussex. They were out doing various dowsing experiments with rods and pendulums when one of their number poked a stick into the ground. A Devil-like form suddenly appeared, complete with horns, and chased these unfortunates down the hill! Then it disappeared.

This kind of Guardian can do no physical harm, but psychologically can scare the crap out of you. If the Guardian's power is not renewed from time to time, it will gradually lose its power and fade out all together. It is like a robot programmed to do what it does, and with great effect.

In 1993, it was suggested that the Centre for Crop Circle Studies might approach the crop circle phenomenon from a psychic point of view, with an angle to actually videoing a formation 'going down.' With so many claims of faking by the likes of Doug and Dave, two pensioners (how the hell they travelled round the world hoaxing hundreds of circles I shall never know), it became increasingly clear that we had to get something on tape. Together, with two fellow psychics, I sat down for a meditation, focusing on finding a suitable spot/field that we might observe. More than that, it had to have an energy line running through it, the reason being that all genuine circles have an earth energy line, fed by an earth energy power site (like Silbury Hill in Wiltshire). Water is always present, usually under the field.

We needed a place that we could observe from without committing trespass. A tall order. During the meditation, Diana and Carole, my fellow psychics, saw a pond surrounded by trees, some of whose roots were actually in the water. (They both saw visions of the Earth Mother). They saw a field just below the pond. I saw the symbol of a devil standing astride a ravine. In one hand he held the number 2, and in the other hand he held the number 7. His belt was made up of the letters J.U.N.E - 27th June! This indicated quite clearly that the pond and field was near a place called Devil's Dyke. The 27th June was the date for the operation!

The next day, I got out my Ordnance Survey map and began to map dowse the Devil's Dyke area, holding in mind the vision of the pond that I had seen also, though my vision showed a path that ran along the back of the pond with a small fence. I found a spot where the pendulum responded very favourably indeed, but there was no water on that part of the map at all and water was most important. There WAS a pond, there HAD to be a pond.

A bunch of us, including my friends from CCCS Sussex, Barry Reynolds and Andy Thomas, set out for Devil's Dyke to hunt the spot indicated on the map. I waited in the car and watched them disappear through bush and scrub, making their way slowly up the hill toward the supposed spot. I waited for about half an hour, when I received a wave of excitement. Something had happened! I watched them make their snail-like pace down the hill and back through the bush and scrub.

Their faces betrayed absolutely nothing. I feared the worst. As Andy approached the car, his face broke into a huge smile - in fact they were all smiling. They had found the pond exactly where we said it would be. It looked down onto a perfect field of barley. And later my nephew Quenton confirmed, through dowsing, that an energy line ran right through the pond, fed by a power point at the Devil's Dyke, and carried on right through our cornfield! It was perfect, down to the last detail.

During all this preparation, Joeb was involved from the very start. His advice was invaluable. He warned us that getting the Devic forces to behave and tolerate our presence was not going to be easy, but he would do what he could. He told us that balls of light would be seen (Devas) plus UFO activity and, he hoped, an 'astrogram' (an astrogram is a pattern of light in the sky). He also warned us not to bring too much electrical equipment, apart from the two camcorders and the odd 'stills' camera. We were to have a ritualistic 'wash' before we began the operation. (I now know that this can be done with the mind). The reason for no excess equipment was to do with the energies that would be released which could cause problems.

About 11 people were chosen for this all night vigil. This turned out to be too many, but it was too late to do anything about it. The time given by Joeb was 2.30am to 4.30am. This was the time that we had to keep watch over our field.

I had to be stretchered up to our point of stay. At one stage, when the lads were having a bit of a breather, Joeb's voice suddenly floated up from the stretcher to say that conditions were perfect and all was well. However, all was not well. There were people present who were not really in harmony with what we were trying to do, although the energy up there on the hill overlooking our field of barley was so strong you could almost touch it! But NOTHING HAPPENED! Yes, balls of light in a circle were seen by some of us, yes, UFO's were spotted by others, yes. But no formation appeared.

I was bitterly disappointed. After being stretchered down the hill and back safely in my car, Quenton and I made for a transport café where we ate a hearty but miserable breakfast. I then went home to bed.

That evening, I received a telephone call from Tony Mezen, a psychic friend of mine who knew nothing about our experiment. He phoned to tell me that at precisely 2.30am on the 27th, he had decided to sit in his garden and watch the sky. From 2.30am to 4.30am (cosmic coincidence?), Tony watched 17 UFOs fly over his house, performing various acrobatics in formation - patterns such as triangles and squares! According to Joeb, Tony was the nearest link to our group and it was no coincidence that he was urged to sit out that night. It was as if we were receiving a message that things could have happened that night, but that we were not ready for them personally. (A much fuller account of all this can be found in *Quest For Contact*.)

Disappointment was the name of the game. But not for long. At least half of those present that night, later experienced psychic and spiritual experiences of their own. Even the sceptics amongst us, though interested parties, began to 'see' things in a different light: They could now accept things into their consciousness that before would have been rejected outright.

Joeb had told us many times that the circles were made by a combination of sound, water and earth energy. The sound was projected from outer space or through the Earth Mother. The crop circles formed were put there to try to change the ways of Mankind. They influenced the surrounding countryside and all those who went near them. Some people's lives have been changed forever! 'Shape Power' is nothing new. The crop circle phenomenon is part of the Earth Changes.

A symbol is very powerful. Shape is very powerful! Has anybody reading this ever tried walking slowly through a sacred maze? Try it. It is a simple geometric shape cut into the earth (sometimes represented by a Bush Maze), but its very shape, and the person's movement THROUGH that shape, creates mind-altering energy! It's like Pyramid power! It's a reality. Yes, the shape of the Great Pyramid of Giza (in miniature) DOES sharpen razor blades, it DOES change milk into yoghurt without adding a culture, it DOES mummify organic matter without purifying! That a mere shape can do that, is amazing. The Universe is made up of geometric shapes and numbers and I don't pretend to understand any of it.

CHAPTER 25

*I*t had been suggested by Michael Green that I might try to contact sacred site Guardians in the Sussex area in the hope that they may help us in our quest to contact the Circlemakers. Guardians come in all shapes and sizes, some human in form, some Devic, some a combination of both!

It was on 12th December 1993 that we first made contact with Emun, Guardian of the ancient hill-fort Cissbury Ring, which overlooks the Sompting area of West Sussex. It was a cold, rainy day with a slight wind, making conditions a little uncomfortable. The idea of dragging me in a wheelchair to the top of Cissbury to channel was abandoned before we even thought about it. Cissbury Ring in winter is no picnic. We settled for the lower Cissbury car-park. Andy Thomas, Martin Noakes, Barry and Linda Reynolds and myself piled into my car which soon steamed up with the crush of bodies. Andy held a *Toys-R-Us* type cassette recorder (all that was available!) to my mouth whilst I tuned in to the Guardian of Cissbury Ring.

As I sat in the car, cassette tape whirling, I wondered what the hell I was letting myself in for. I had never tried to channel a Guardian before. What would it be like? I didn't have long to wait. The customary rhythmic deep breathing began to gather strength, the tingle of energy around my head and arms. Inwardly I was thinking: so far, so good. He came on strong then.

Playing the tape back later, I heard the Guardian speak very quietly, but with authority. His first words were "What do you want?" as if we'd disturbed him. Very cautiously, questions were asked by the others concerning crop circles. He told us that he knew of them, but that they were not of his doing. He and two other Guardians at Cissbury worked as a trinity and were concerned only with keeping the energy lines clear. When asked whether he could help us in our quest, he said that he would do what he could. That was it! Barry, sitting directly behind me, had to stop himself from falling asleep as my body drew on his own personal energy. This is not an unusual phenomena; many folk who attend psychic sittings sit around yawning their heads off, and not, I'm pleased to say, because they're bored (well, not everyone, that is)!

On February 13th 1994, we again contacted Emun, who turned out to be the spokesman for the three Guardians at Cissbury. The other two Guardians were female: Tryst, who represented the Earth Mother, and Rachael (this name may not be correct, but it is as near as I can get), who represented the Sun. Emun represented the Moon. This time we sat in the relative comfort of my sitting room. Michael Green was also with us.

Because I had already contacted Emun, it was not hard for him to come through again away from Cissbury Ring, time and space being meaningless. Again, he spoke quietly, a little more friendly and amiable.

Prior to this sitting, I had been receiving information regarding Cissbury Ring that made no sense: I was being shown the belly of a naked woman. There was nothing sexual about it, but I knew that Cissbury Ring and this female form were linked. I searched the Ordnance Survey map for some name that might represent the belly or navel of a woman. Nothing came remotely near. The next image was of a temple that I was told once stood on top of Cissbury Ring. I got an aerial map of the Ring: it had the shapely form of a woman! And sure enough, the dowsing pendulum indicated very strongly that the temple I sought was indeed almost exactly on the navel or belly button!

I asked David Russell to confirm my findings. Not only did he confirm it, but he found that the temple (to Diana) was built on top of a far more ancient site where once stood a 12 foot tall sarsen stone. Although this was questionable, we dowsed that this was as long ago as 8000 years! It would appear that the old stone, which I named the 'Navel Stone', was broken up by the Romans and used as a foundation for the later temple. It was this stone that Emun referred to when he made his second 'appearance'.

He told us that he and the other Guardians used to serve the old Chieftains and Shamans of long ago when they would sit around the Navel Stone as part of a sacred ritual. Part of their work, he said, was weather control and care of crops. But they also helped set up communication with "the Gods". He went on to tell us that we could make contact with a higher intelligence that would be able to help us in our quest via the Fifth energy band of the etheric remnants of the standing stone.

This is one of the seven bands of spiral energy that most dowsers are familiar with. They are in accord with the seven Chakras, or power centres, of the human body. The Fifth band, going up, is the band of communication, corresponding with the throat Chakra of the body. This contact would have to take place on 28th June between 2.00pm and 4.00pm.

Later on, I was told that I had to find the precise height of the Fifth band, mark it on a wooden pole, fix an amethyst crystal on the top and place it precisely where the old Navel stone used to stand. Meanwhile, David Russell, Andy, Barry and Martin went aloft to Cissbury to find the exact location of the stone. They found it, marked it and photographed it so as to find it again quickly on 28th June.

On 29th May, our team set out to track down two more Guardians in our locality to see if they could be of any further help. We spoke with Cened, a Celtic Warrior whose jurisdiction was the Sompting fields around the church of St Mary's (site of many Sussex crop formations), and Armis, a Grecian lady based in the Lancing College area, whose task was the protection and inspiration of "education", appropriately enough. Both said that they would do what they could to clear the energy lines for our big day, but that was all they could promise.

The day arrived: 28th June 1994. It was without doubt the most beautiful day of the summer so far, very hot, but with enough breeze to make it bearable. There were eight of us, including myself: Michael Green, Barry Reynolds, Andy Thomas, Linda Reynolds, Karen Douglas, David Russell and Martin Noakes. From an inner directive, I was urged to ask my fellow 'questers' to each represent the seven Kingdoms of Nature: earth, air, fire, water, animal vegetable and mineral. Each were given their respective element; I would then take my place in their midst with my hand on top of the crystal on the pole marking the Navel Stone. The part that nobody relished, including myself, was pushing Bura to the top in a wheelchair. We needn't have worried. The earth was dry and a clear path enabled Barry and Martin to push me up with no trouble at all. The Guardians were indeed with us.

On my way to Cissbury in my car, I desperately wanted to clear my mind of pre-conceived thoughts. Instead of listening to the *Enigma Variations* which tends to open me up to higher things, I whacked on some early rock 'n' roll: Little Richard. I arrived at Cissbury to the sound of 'Tutti Frutti' and 'Long Tall Sally'! I was ready!

We found the spot and put the pole and crystal in place. Four other crystals were placed on the four cardinal points, thus creating a huge medicine-wheel, to create as much balance from our side as we could.

At roughly 2.15pm, we began. Although Cissbury Ring is well-known as THE place to walk the dog or just spend a summer's day, not one soul disturbed us or came into view. No-one came near. Were Emun and his team helping us even now?

I sat before the pole, facing north. The others sat around, forming a circle. I made an opening prayer, giving thanks, under God, to the three Guardians for setting the whole thing up. Then I put my hand on the crystal and waited. At first I felt nothing. Almost without warning, I felt a surge of energy. The muscles in my jaw tightened, my breathing deepened... and suddenly I was speaking - that is, SOMETHING was!

The small cassette recorder on my lap and the video camera beside me picked up a voice of extreme authority and power. The 'transmission'

Michael Green-(Chairman of C.C.C.S.)-wires me for sound atop Cissbury Ring for the Transmission from Sirius

lasted about ten minutes. After it was all over I collapsed into tears. I was neither unhappy nor joyful. It was just a huge release. I shook for another ten minutes. Michael also took part of the surge which made him feel a little unwell. But we both recovered quickly.

For myself, I can honestly say that I have never before experienced such intensity of power and energy. Never! The only negative after-effect was a slight headache in the evening. What follows is a word-for-word transcript of the transmission that took place on Cissbury Ring, 28th June 1994:

"Greetings, greetings. It has been a long time since we have communicated here, a long time.

I understand your frustration concerning the corn circles - but the frustration will continue, because of those who will not accept. You have asked that circles be performed, created, that cannot be tampered with. We have done this, we have done this. But do not think it will be easy for you to use your equipment to film such an event. It is so difficult because of all the various elemental forces necessary to come together for this occasion and to get them to behave. We would like this, but you know - you all know - that 'they' will not believe you even if this were possible. No.

You have to accept that power comes from circles. The reason that they are here is because your Earth now needs to change. The knowledge of this we have known for thousands of years and we have hinted at it through various mediums and channels for so long, so long. DO NOT PLACE SUCH IMPORTANCE ON THE PROOF! You are expanding. All those who are associated with these circles are expanding now and this is only the beginning. You will have proof with the corn but who will really believe you? You can turn the world upside down and they will not believe you.

But the spirit of the land rises and blossoms and there will be signs in the sky. You will see this. We hope it will be this year that you will see this. But you will. And they will still not believe. But what does it matter? The circles are here to help with this so-called 'rising of the Earth'. She must rise up now and join us. She is like a child to us in space, a jewel and she is waiting to flourish, to become who she really is and to take you all with her. It is such a journey - such a fantastic journey! - and you are part of that journey and you must ride with her. You understand what I am saying to you? You must ride with her and keep the love of God, whatever you conceive that energy to be, in your heart and keep it alive - KEEP IT ALIVE! And the beauty will continue. Lights in the sky. More corn circles. But there is only so much that we can do, only so much. You say they are miracles - yes, we ARE miracle workers - but there are limits. We cannot change the mind of Man. He must do that. You, my friends here, all changed to what you were, and it is only the beginning of vast changes.

(Michael: "Friend, who are you?") *"Trying to get a name through this channel... Jeuz. J-E-U-Z. Jeuz. I am not of human form. I am not. But similar, similar. Sirius. Dog Star. Yes."*

(Michael: "What is your role with us who are part of the Ascension process?") *"The influence that we are giving. Beings such as we are surround the Earth, giving inspiration and support to all those who seek the Light. That is our job, yes, that is it. We have been around for a long time, during great civilisations upon this Earth. I am a spokesman. I have not spoken for a long time. I have come to tell you not to place too much importance on trivia, of trying to prove this or that. It is happening, yes it is happening and will continue."*

"Energy going now. Energy going now."

(Michael: "Thank you for coming to speak with us.") *"It is my pleasure to all of you here - ALL of you here - blessings from us. From us we send you our love. Please continue to work in the Light. Please do this, not for yourself but for the whole of the Earth for she is beautiful, far more beautiful than you will know. But given time you will know how beautiful she is. Continue with your work, but do not be bogged down by trying to prove this or that because in the end IT MAKES NO DIFFERENCE - none! Bless you. Thank you."*

A more detailed account of this story can be found in *Quest For Contact*.

CHAPTER 26

*F*urther back in this book, I mentioned that there were seven chakras in the human body and seven main lines of chakric energy that make up an earth energy line. These split up into many sub-lines, depending on what information is being fed into the grid. The lower three main chakras ie: the first, or Base Chakra, is for survival, self-preservation, hunting, the feeling of being 'grounded' and close to the Earth. The second is the Sexual Chakra, associated with procreation and linked quite closely with the Base Chakra. The third chakra is the solar plexus, the place of the emotions (anger, greed, the need to possess, etc.) and the will. These are energy lines used when violence is present, when war is perpetrated. This does not mean that these three chakras are negative. Absolutely not! When the fourth chakra, the Heart Centre, the great balancer, is in play, together with the fifth (throat: communication), the sixth (third eye: clairvoyance) and the seventh (the Crown Chakra: the releaser, where all the other energies are channelled and processed), then balance is the order of the day.

In 1976, Colin Bloy, master dowser and healer, discovered by psychic means, the Cathar Grail Stone in a cave at Andorra near Arinsal. A Grail Stone is usually a crystal and acts like the memory of a computer, having been programmed with certain esoteric information. This stone, when dowsed, gave information from the 'Elohim' (creator gods) concerning the bringing in of an eighth energy band to replace the old seven band system. This was all to do with the raising of the frequency of the Earth Mother (Ayesha). This eighth chakra represented the Cosmic Overself, the self that enables the Earth to open up to higher beings, higher intelligence, waiting to instruct and help us.

Colin Bloy, Michael Bentine and ten others had to assemble at the ruins of Glastonbury Abbey and perform a sacred ritual at the site of King Arthur's grave. This was done in accordance with the Elohim and was performed with great love and respect. After the ritual was at an end, a main energy line was checked. It now had EIGHT lines! These, of course, would now be in multiples of 16, 32, 64 etc. The higher or finer number of lines would mean greater access to esoteric knowledge. But no-one knew for sure. These lines, or 'courier lines' as I call them because they are 'bringers and receivers' of information, make up an earth energy line (Telluric energy line or main energy line) and these lines of communication were hurtling toward a greater reality.

Colin reasoned that he was fooling himself. He needed proof from a fellow master dowser in another part of the world. Whilst in the Middle East, Colin contacted an old friend, a dowser of many years experience, and invited him to dowse a known main energy line. He asked his friend whether THIS time he would dowse for not just seven lines but eight! His astonished friend thought he had gone a little crazy, but humoured him. Colin watched with bated breath as the dowsing rods began to swing to each section of the energy line... five... six... seven... then eight! The look of total surprise on his friend's face was all Colin needed. It was now an established fact.

As a point of interest, all sacred sites are in the earth grid system, whether they be Muslim, Christian, Buddhist, Hindu, Jewish, Celtic, whatever. Sadly, the ceaseless chatter of powerful men, like politicians also feed into it! Surely this gives credence to 'right thought, right speech and right action.' Minding our 'Ps and Qs' takes on a whole different concept. Nowhere can anybody hide from self.... or the Earth's courier lines!

At one point, I received information, thrust upon me before sleep, that in 1999 the eight line system will go up to a nine line system! I was wrong about that, very wrong. To date there is a 13 line system and fully activated! However, the ninth chakra is multi-dimensional and will allow higher beings even easier access to Earth. It has been suggested that more UFOs will be seen and many more will land. It will be well into the next century that all 18 courier lines will be in full operation! Colin Bloy says that there are 16 to master before we finally merge with the Eternal. My information is that there are 18 (but who's counting?) which will at last bring us home, or at least a step or three nearer the source. Then the Earth, together with Mankind, will have truly risen.

Unfortunately, or fortunately, there was more to come. I mentioned my vision of a nine line system to David Russell. He looked at me with surprise: "But it's been a TEN line system since 1987?" "What?" I almost shouted, "I don't understand. I received that information involuntarily. I didn't ask for it. When I receive information like that it's usually correct. I just don't understand." David went on to explain that the eight line system had gone up to a ten line system in 1987 after the Harmonic Conversion world link-up where people from all over the Earth tuned in at a certain time to bring light to the planet. From that moment on, the Earth had a ten line system.

Now I was REALLY confused. Why would I get information if it was total rubbish? Maybe it was total rubbish and I was being conned; after all, this psychic stuff is not exactly an exact science. Was I being messed about? (About this time, I received information, again just before I slept, concerning the late Peter Cushing, who wished me to convey a message to Michael Bentine to tell him that everything that Michael had told him regarding life after death was true. When Michael - who has since himself passed - was informed about the message from Peter Cushing, he said that he had only met Peter once and all they talked about was *life after death!*) But what of the information I had received concerning the crop circle experiments, and the information that led to the communication with Jeuz on top of Cissbury Ring? All entirely accurate and mainly unasked for!

What to do, what to do? I phoned a dowser friend of mine, Hilda Bell, who had no axe to grind concerning earth energy lines. I asked her if she would dowse the lines of a typical main energy line and to let me know about lines nine and 10. Two hours later, she phoned me back and told me that line nine was only working on 20% and line 10 was not working at all! This was what I needed to know. The 10 lines were 'in place' but nine and 10 were not activated, that is line nine was only just operating! She confirmed also that line nine would be 100% operational in 1999. Two other dowsers confirmed this. But I wasn't satisfied. I needed to hear it from David Russell, a man of great dowsing experience whom I respected very much. I phoned him and asked him to check out these findings. "Hang on, I'll do it now," he said. I waited with fingers crossed. I could see him in my mind's eye, his crystal pendulum whirling its information. "You're absolutely right," he said, "except I get between 20 and 25% on line nine!" It's that sort of fine accuracy that I had come to expect from David! The relief I felt at hearing that confirmation was extreme to say the least. "Thanks, David, I really needed to hear that from you."

As most of you the know, the aura of a human being is the reflection of the physical, mental and spiritual aspect and can be 'read' by the colours that emanate from the aura, plus the 'feelings' one gets from being close to a person. Similarly, the aura of personality of, say, a town is made up of the collective thoughts and feelings of the people who live in that town and these thoughts and feelings are caught up into the earth energy grid, thereby giving out the feeling or personality of that town. Not only that, but the whole personality or persona of what makes us, for instance, English is expressed in the same way. In other words, our essential 'Britishness' is held in these lines in much the same way that an object which has been in the possession of someone will hold all the information about that person which can be tapped by means of touch clairvoyance or psychometry (as in the Al Bowly incident). Just as one's emotion can be tapped, or one's sexuality, or one's creativity and spirituality, so then can the courier lines, opening up to what is happening at any given time.

A harpsichord player friend of mine once gave a recital. Before he started to play, I dowsed him seated at his instrument, with his permission, of course. I found nothing. Within minutes of his playing, a line was dowsed that went right through my friend and his harpsichord, which remained for three to four days before fading. His own personal built-in line of musical inspiration reached out to the nearest earth courier line and tapped the *aspect* of the courier line carrying inspiration and creativity... or did the line reach out to *him?* I'm not sure. It's a curious thing, but when there is a total eclipse of the Moon, ALL of the energy lines disappear. Hmmm. If a terrible deed has been done at a certain place, like a murder or rape, or at the scene of a bloody battle, the vibrations generated there are held in the energy grid until such time as they fade or are 'cleared out' or 'cleansed' by a site Guardian or human being trained in this art. A skilled person with an 'iron will' and total positivity will just 'ask' and it will be done!

CHAPTER 27

*I*am of the opinion that not only are crop circles created by sound projected from outer space by space beings who are here to help us with the raising of the Earth's frequency level, but there are 'Permanent Energy Patterns' that have been in place for thousands of years, where once stood stone representatives of those patterns.

For some years, I had felt that certain crop circles were formed where ancient places of power once were, and that those same stone circles/complexes were built on already existing patterns of sacred geometry, patterns that could only have been found by dowsing or clairvoyance. These patterns created, by shape alone, a type of energy used for the maintenance of the Earth and Man and Woman kind, cradling them in a cosmic balance so rare and fine that we can only guess at the harmony that existed then, perhaps hundreds of thousands of years ago, not even a blip in cosmic time.

As is now well established, we know that crop circles are fed by lines coming from major earth energy sources like Cissbury Ring, Wolstonbury Hill, the Rollright Stones and Avebury. There is usually water running underneath the site in much the same way that pre-reformation churches are generally built on old power sites used by the ancients. We also know that sound is very important. Think of ANY major religion where ceremony is performed and you will find that sound always plays a great part in raising the energy of ceremony, even some of the weirder sects.

A group of us from CCCS Sussex had been involved in several attempts to interact with the circle-making force in previous years. So the idea formed that in 1995 we would try to trigger one of these earth energy patterns into forming a crop circle by pouring energy into the grid ourselves.

What I needed to do was to find a site that had an etheric pattern already there, a corn field that was already fed by an earth energy line with water underneath. I map-dowsed the local area and came up with a site at Saddlescombe, near Pyecombe, just west of the A23. I got David Russell to check my findings and he confirmed that it was a Place of Power. Although on a slope, it was a fine cornfield.

Next, we had to contact the Spirit Guardian of Wolstonbury Hill from where the earth energy line was fed. Wolstonbury Hill, overlooking Hurstpierpoint in West Sussex, is well known as a place of great energy, and is very beautiful, full of mystery and magic. Jason Porthouse and I set off for Wolstonbury one day in February. We drove to the bottom of the hill, parked the car and sat there. As Jason was a novice channeller (and getting better all the time) I suggested that he too 'open up' to try to contact the Guardian. It was a struggle. The Guardian had a couple of goes at connecting. In the end he made it and my face took on a very broad smile. Jason felt him too and that smile was the 'signature' of the being we came to know as 'Damus'.

Jason questioned him and asked him whether he would help us in our quest to bring down a crop circle that was fed by an energy line that came from Wolstonbury Hill. He said that he would be delighted! I could feel the joy in him, as if he were a child that had been kept in and then was let out again to play with the human beings that he had not played/worked with for many hundreds of years, perhaps thousands. He would help us all he could, but could guarantee nothing. From that moment on, whenever Jason or I went near the Wolstonbury Hill area, Damus would make a friendly 'grab' at us and we would feel his gleeful presence and a large smile would appear on our faces as he grew close. God knows what our passengers thought: "What the hell are you smiling about?" they would say. "Oh nothing, just thinking about someone I know."

Andy Thomas, Barry Reynolds and Martin Noakes already knew what was in the air and gave their full support. Michael Green was notified, together with other trusted members of CCCS Sussex who were in on the Cissbury Ring 'Transmission from Sirius' on June 28th 1994 (as told in *Quest For Contact*). A date was set for us to congregate at my place in Lancing to have a serious talk with Damus and to hear from him what should be our duties concerning the stimulation of the earth energy line that ran through our chosen site.

About a month later, we all gathered to hear what Damus had to say and we were not disappointed. He came through beaming and smiling and expressed how happy he was to be "working with humans again." He gave us a brief history as to how he was chosen to be Guardian of the 'Whistling Hill'. (Damus's name for Wolstonbury Hill. He said that in times past, when the wind was in a certain direction the hill whistled, but now with the new roads and development around it, it was a rare event). He was a Druid, he said, but that was not what they were really called. He said the word was nearer to 'Drood', not Druid, and anyway it was a collective name for many priesthoods in England at that time. He was chosen to take over from the Guardian before he died in the earthly sense. It was a very great honour and he was delighted to accept. He had to 'strike the oak' six times to complete his promise that he would serve the area known as Wolstonbury.

Damus was asked what we needed to do in order to pour as much energy down the line as we could. He said that crystals should be held which would amplify the energy. He also told us that the use of sound was very important. Prior to our meeting with Damus, I had dowsed out a chord of music that would, perhaps, resonate with the natural sound that each of the eight sections, or courier lines, of a main energy line possessed; ie: the first courier line is C natural, the second D natural, the third E natural, and so on. The chord that I dowsed out was: A, B flat, C sharp, D, F and G sharp. This was recorded and played for Damus to hear. He approved. A proper studio sound was later produced using only pure tones. The sound was eerie, but very mystical (later, folk were to say that the sound was very like the sound that had been heard many times around crop circles). Damus was asked on what date we were to proceed. He told us: "The last new moon in June, at sunset." Sunset and dawn are powerful times, when the elemental forces and Devas are at their strongest. So we had the 28th June... again, a date which had figured strongly in previous experiments.

By now, I was beginning to lose him, or he was beginning to lose me. At one stage I lost him altogether. After about a minute, he returned. It was a strain to hold on to him and he said his goodbyes, but told us that he was at our disposal. What a nice man. Damus is tall with a very large, kindly face, a huge beard and long hair. And, yes, he was wearing a long white robe! He also carried a very long staff in his right hand that had a symbol of a half moon at its top.

Barry Reynolds, on hearing the structure of the chord of music, took a biro and sketched a hypothetical crop pattern. It turned out to be exactly the same as the resulting corn circles which would follow. Exactly!

Meanwhile, back in the psychic workshop, I decided that I would seek out the help of one Jan Linch, a healer who uses colour and crystals in her work. We both knew that each courier line that made up a major earth energy line corresponded in colour with the chakric centres in the human body, as we are, every one of us, linked into the earth energy grid whether we like it or not. Not only were the colours the same and the sound vibrations the same, but we also chose crystals that resonated for each courier line and human chakra. It would take too long to go into detail as to what represented what, but the correctly corresponding crystals were found.

And so began a very long wait. Keeping the whole thing a secret was always difficult, but necessary. Meanwhile, Jason and Andy went and checked out the site of Saddlescombe to see where we could best sit on the slopes of Wolstonbury. A route was finally found that would enable us to get somewhere near the top of the hill where easy access was available for a bloke being wheeled up a mountain. Namely me! Sadly, we couldn't actually see the field in question, but were assured by Jason, no mean dowser, that the line to which we were to lend the weight of our bottoms ran directly through it. I also decided that this year I would *write* an invocation instead of uttering one off the top of my head.

Then came the part that shifted my perspective. I got a call from my old friend Tony Mezen, a fellow psychic, who had received information for me, at two in the morning, the day before the experiment, from someone calling herself Elle. "Do you know who Elle is?" I asked him. "No," he said, "I just got the name Elle." I told Tony that Elle or Ellen is one of the names of the Earth Spirit and that Lady Ellen was once my pet name for Gaia. Tony read the message out to me over the phone whilst I wrote it down. This is what it said:

"I am your Wyvern. It is the top, not level nor rocky, but earth on top. That is where Elle sleeps. But a warning: do not wake Elle without magic iron. Bring song and word. But not when the sun sleeps, only in the light. Bring fire and water. Fire without soot, water without mud. Pure fire. Pure water. Earth and air are as they are. Move where the path leads. Only three, no more. One staff, three stones. Many lie there, with marks, without marks. Between two..." The message ended abruptly.

This hit me right in the solar plexus. I knew I had to make sense of it. I KNEW it was a reference to the 28th, the next day! Tony had no idea of what we were intending, no idea that we were engaging in any sort of experiment... let alone the next day!

I read the message over the phone to Andy. I then asked him whether the description of *"It is the top, not level or rocky, but earth on top"* fitted where we were going on the evening of the 28th. He said it wasn't at the top, but as high as we could get with a wheelchair. It was indeed 'not level or rocky.' The 'earth on top' he wasn't sure about. I told him that I was taking this message seriously and that I felt that when this message said 'Only three, no more. One staff' that this referred to Jason, Andy and myself. The staff was Damus! I told Andy not to worry, I'd sort it out.

The reference to a 'Wyvern' was significant. A Wyvern is a mythical and Heraldic animal resembling a dragon. Dragon or serpent energy is very often used to describe earth energy, or indeed *Kundalini* energy. I charged some water to purify it, then left it out in the sun for all of that day and the next. The reference to 'three stones' was to my mind, perhaps, three stones that we would find at the top of the hill and decided to wait and see for myself. Meanwhile I got together an agate Fire Stone to represent the 'Fire without soot' (the fire that does not burn), for the 'iron' I used a rare Iron Stone or Bungie Stone that had been given to me by Tony many months before. I wrote another invocation for just the three of us and knew that this small ceremony with the Fire Stone and the Iron Stone and the purified water must be performed BEFORE the full invocation and main activity of the whole group.

I didn't have long to wait. The 28th arrived. We all met up in the *Jack and Jill* pub car park, much to the annoyance of the landlord. We promised we'd be back for a beer or three later, after we had a walk! Then we took two cars to the first gate up the hill of Wolstonbury. I was then transferred to the wheelchair where we made our way to the target or 'transmission area'. Those involved were Michael Green, David Russell, Martin Noakes, Barry Reynolds and his wife Linda, Karen Douglas and her partner, Steve Alexander (who, in fact, manned the video camera much further down the hill covering our chosen field), Andy Thomas, Jason Porthouse and myself.

Earlier in the day I had received a call from Jason, whose job it was to dowse out which person should sit on what courier line. He had a problem. For some reason he could not fathom, Karen was not supposed to sit on any of the eight lines. Jason asked me to check this. I got the same result. This was insane. Karen was a lovely lady and perfect for the job. How could we tell this sweet lady that she should not sit? Jason phoned Andy, who suggested she sit on the number nine courier line! Now, we weren't originally going to use number nine because it was not fully activated, only working at 25%. However, we dowsed this out and got a very firm 'Yes'. I had to hurriedly come up with another crystal for her as Jason had found that I too must sit on a line, namely number eight. I had thought that I was to sit apart in case Damus wished to say something. That was not to be. Later on, of course, I found out why we had to use the number nine courier Line.

On reaching the top, just before the last gate, we stopped to rest and look around. The wind was so strong up there that you could hardly hear each other speak; it was also very cold, even though down at ground level it was, or had been, over 70 degrees. We just weren't dressed for it. Andy lent me his sweater. I noticed that we were standing between three tumuli, two on one side of the path and one or more on the other. I knew there and then that this was where *'many lie there. With marks, without marks. Between two...'* I knew this was the place where we must start the proceedings, Jason, Andy and I. This was *'where Elle sleeps'*: the sleeping dragon (energy), the life energy of Gaia herself. The tumuli carried the remains of the ancient ones. Perhaps these burial mounds were once marked with stones, now fallen and carried away.

Time was running in all directions and the sun was making a rapid descent before it would melt in its own crucible to be cast once again to ring the changes for the next day. We intended to start the main proceedings at 8.45pm, as the sun set. Meanwhile, David Russell had marked out the nine courier lines for us all to sit on. David found that each line went in the opposite direction to the other, alternately, though we didn't then understand why. One flowed toward our field, the next would flow the other way. Michael Green checked David's findings and found them sound. Each was allocated their particular crystal and told that at the given time they were to open their Crown Chakra (like a flower opening on the top of the head) and bring down the golden light of the 'Christ consciousness', take it into their bodies, then let it stream out through their solar plexus and into their crystal and thus into the ground in front of them. This we would do for 30 minutes from sunset.

At about 8.20pm, Andy, Jason and myself made our way to the burial mounds. To Andy I gave the purified water to sprinkle on the mound, or very near it, as we couldn't get beyond the fence, at least not with a wheelchair! To Jason I gave the Iron Stone. For my part, I had the Fire Stone plus a small written invocation to Lady Ellen (or Ayesha, as Joeb calls her). The three of us crowded near the edge of the mound. I read the invocation. I felt the strong presence of Damus. At a given point, Jason buried his Iron Stone. Then it was my turn to bury the Fire Stone, after which Andy sprinkled the area with the holy water. (As I understand it the Iron and Fire stones formed an alchemical process. The two elements, a cocktail of two frequencies, needed a catalyst to release the energy they produced. The catalyst was the 'charged' water.)

Damus came on strong then. I felt him raise his staff and plunge it into the earth. After a few minutes, we made our way back to the others. "I don't know what you did over there, Paul," said David Russell, "but the lines have shot up in number from nine to 18 and then up to 27." Something was happening!

The sun began to set, so I read the main invocation that I had worked on days before. We called on Lord Michael, Lord of the Angels of Light and mediator between the human race and the Devic forces. We made our request for their co-operation with our project and that a positive result would be granted. I asked that Damus would be supported in his work and that we be guided and sustained and that all this be done in the name of Light, so be it. Damus came through then and had us start the proceedings. It was 8.47pm. The musical chord played constantly and seemed perfect for the job. *'Bring song and word'*; we had done that. *'Not when the sun sleeps'* (at night); we had done that. No-one pretended that meditating in that high wind was easy but at 9.10pm, Damus brought the proceedings to a close. I felt a lot of energy and so did Michael Green, but we were so cold. David Russell did a spot dowse. The lines had now risen to 72! We came down the hill full of hope, but expected nothing. I was cold and tired and went straight home to bed.

The next day I waited for the phone to ring. Nothing happened! I thought to myself: another psychic dead-end? That night Damus paid me a call: "You have done far more than you know. The number nine courier line has now risen from 25 per cent up to 45 per cent. I glimpsed Lady Ellen. She told me about three circles that had been formed. She was smiling warmly". I was tired and wanted to sleep. But this was so strong. The next morning I woke refreshed and immediately dowsed the ninth energy line. It had risen from 25 per cent to between 40 and 45 per cent. I couldn't believe it!

I tried to phone David to check it out. I left a message on Jason's answering machine to dowse it out. I phoned fellow dowser Hilda Bell and asked her to check it out also. Then came the phone call! A crop circle had gone down at Felbridge, near East Grinstead, near the A22. According to Barry Reynolds, it connected in a straight line to Wolstonbury Hill and our site at Saddlescombe. I needed this confirmed. Then I got my first call back from Hilda. She confirmed it. The energy had risen to at least 40 per cent. Jason phoned in. He got between 40 and 45 per cent! Meanwhile David had got the correct map readings from Barry and confirmed that the crop circle was connected to the energy line that we had meditated in, but that it had GONE DOWN IN THE OPPOSITE DIRECTION! The energy we sent had gone not to Saddlescombe, but to Felbridge!

The farmer was extremely friendly and so were his staff. Another plus was the fact that I could, for once, drive my car to within 50 yards of the formation thanks to a mown strip around the edge of the field. The farmer told us that he had visited the field on Monday and Tuesday and one of his men had checked it on the Wednesday (28th June) and there was no formation. But on Thursday morning there it was – it had appeared the night of our experiment! After David had told me his findings I asked him to check the number nine line. David got 40 per cent! I asked to check whether this was global. I heard him mutter "You bugger!" He told me that the pendulum swung backwards and forwards, which meant neither yes or no. Jason tried it and got the same effect, but when asked whether the energy was spreading around the grid he got a 'yes', and so did I.

I kept wondering about Lady Ellen and the THREE circles. Perhaps the others would appear soon or had just not been found yet. Barry Reynolds had already suggested beforehand that he believed the six notes in the chord that I had dowsed out might result in the shape he had sketched. He phoned to tell me this indeed corresponded with the six rings and circles found in the formation, each ring being of a different size and resonance! I asked Barry to tell me, as I hadn't had a chance to visit it yet, what the formation looked like. He described THREE SEPARATE

RINGED CIRCLES riding due East West. "Did you say three SEPARATE rings? I mean, not superimposed on one another?" "That's right," he said, "one ring at the top, a second ring in the middle containing a single ring within it, and a third circle containing two rings!" "So that's what she meant!" I almost shouted. "She meant three crop circles IN THE SAME FIELD!" I wasn't going barmy after all (that's a matter of opinion, I hear you scream).

For my money this put the lid on our success; we had three circles that corresponded in size to six circular sound elements, the sound that we played during that wild windy time atop Wolstonbury Hill and forseen by Barry. This was our formation.

After all these years of attempted interaction, it seemed that at least one of the Circle Makers had taken us into their confidence. That Circle Maker was the Earth Mother herself. Perhaps it just took patience and trust, mixed with dedication and love, to come up with the right formula. Whatever it was, we owed it all to forces outside of us who seem intent on plying us with knowledge... a tiny piece at a time.

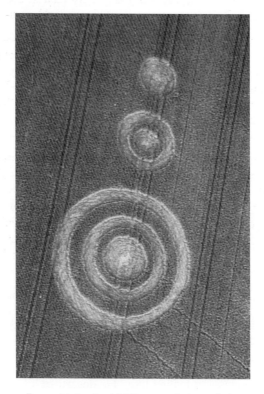

The crop circle formation at Felbridge, as a result of our meditation.

CHAPTER 28

*T*ony Mezen first told me about the staff that he was making at the beginning of June 1995. "It's made of apple wood, decorated with crystals and rune stones. I seem to be guided every step of the way. *I'm not designing it, but somebody is.* I don't even know what it's for, I only know that it's not me who will use it!" It was intriguing, but as far as I was concerned that was as far as it went.

Tony had helped me in the past. Totally unconsciously, he gave me information when I needed it and usually when my mind was focused too hard on a project for me to let in any other information. For the Wolstonbury project, Tony had given me information at the eleventh hour that was invaluable in helping me and the other members of the Centre for Crop Circle Studies in raising the number nine courier line of the earth energy grid from 25 per cent activity to over 46 per cent globally. This allowed higher knowledge, kept from Mankind for many thousands of years, to filter into our consciousness to help us unfold and give some idea as to where we are going, all part of the Earth ascension process. Many groups of dedicated people are working, world-wide, to this effect.

Tony phoned me on July 10th to tell me that he was working flat out on the staff and that it was nearly completed. There seemed to be some negative forces that kept tripping him up, trying to delay him or get him to stop all together. Tony told me that all the people who had held the staff during its creation had remarked how light it was. "The person who says that the staff is heavy is the one to use it," he said, "but I still don't know what it's for."

Tony's sister, Sylvia, one of the founder members of our group, phoned me. "I have some information from Tony, can I come and see you?" At 2.00pm on July 17th, Sylvia came to see me. She told me that the staff was now ready, apart from a few details: two small silver bottles, one containing sacred ash, the other holy water, to be attached to the staff on the day of the ceremony... whatever that ceremony was! Sylvia showed me a quotation, written in July 1881, by Mahatma Koot Hoomi. It read as follows:

"For countless generations hath the adept builded a fane (church/temple) of imperishable rocks, a giant's tower of infinite thought, wherein the Titan (large and strong, notable for outstanding achievement) dwelt, and will yet, if need be, dwell alone, emerging from it, but at the end of every cycle, to invite the elect of Mankind to co-operate with him and to help in his turn enlighten superstitious man."

Tony had come across this quotation from the writings of Lord Koot Hoomi and it struck him that this was important and referred to the staff. Again, he didn't know why, but had the urge to get this message to me via Sylvia. After reading it, I looked up the word Titan. Apart from its obvious connection ie: 'very large and/or strong', it is also notable for 'outstanding achievement'. The 'fane' is a church or temple where dwells the 'infinite thought'. The invitation to Mankind to co-operate with Him will help 'enlighten superstitious Man'. All this information bounced in and out of my brain. I decided I ought to see Tony and the staff as soon as possible. Sylvia phoned to see whether he was in. He was. We arrived 15 minutes later.

Tony brought the staff for me to see. We were seated in his front garden with traffic pounding past along the Brighton Road... The staff was eight foot long and very beautiful. The apple wood was almost pure white and it was elegantly encrusted with carefully made rune stones and crystals. The rune stones were carved in wood, with the sign of each rune burned into each piece. There were nine runes in all, plus a further six which were to be kept aside for six chosen people during and after the ceremony. The handle was bound in leather (not to my moral taste, but it seems that earth, air, fire, water, animal, vegetable and mineral had to be present... plus the eighth: the spirit.) and at the top of the handle was a carefully placed rose quartz crystal. Tony handed the staff to me.

I took it in both hands and the first thing I said was "Gosh, it's heavier than I thought!" As the words came out of my mouth I realised what I had said. "You're the one then," said Tony, "you're the one that has to use it. Everybody else had said how light it was." Now I already *knew* what other people had said and I was determined not to say anything other than the truth and the truth was: to me it was heavy! I also didn't *want* to be 'the one'. I had been involved with quite a few psychic quests in the last few years and I felt it was about time somebody else had a go.

As I held the staff, a wave of emotion came over me. I couldn't speak. Tears came. I had to wait for that moment to subside. Tony handed me a tissue. "I think I have someone who wants to speak to us," I said. Before the emotion started, I had been telling Tony and Sylvia about a vision of St George and the dragon and how the lance of St George had pierced the heart of the dragon and that I felt this was relevant; the piercing, or opening up, of dragon, or earth energy.

I asked that we bring up, through visualisation, a protective and balancing pyramid around us before I started to 'tune in'. Within no time at all, the customary deep breathing began and Lord Koot Hoomi began to speak. Koot Hoomi had first spoken to our group (as he has to many thousands of groups throughout the world) at our first 'White Light Celebration' two years earlier, which marked our first year as a group. He had also spoken to us at the second White Light Celebration, and on occasion throughout the year. I think that this time, sitting in that front garden with all the traffic thundering past, he was as powerful as I'd ever known him.

He thanked Tony for his work on the staff and for following instructions to the letter. He told us that the staff was to be used to open the Earth's energy grid even wider and that the staff was an alchemical device of great power. The staff was to be used in ceremony and placed into the Heart Chakra line of the Earth Mother. When the ceremony was at an end, the staff must be buried and left for the Earth Mother to take Herself. He said that this was an act of pure love. That was as much as I could remember. I knew that the staff had now been fully charged, Koot Hoomi had told us that much, and that NO-ONE must touch it before its use. Tony carefully wrapped the staff in cloth. Physically, there was no way I could do it and I knew that it was okay for Tony to touch it. He did, after all, build it. "It's yours now, Paul," said Tony, "you take it home with you."

Before all this happened I had made arrangements with David Russell to book the 12th century St James's Church at Ashurst, West Sussex, on the 12th August so that our group could all come together and join in the World-wide Healing Project that was now well underway. I couldn't think of a better place than a pre-reformation church, a place of power, to give out to the Earth Mother (Ayesha). Sadly, there was a wedding on, but as David's house was right next door to the church, with its own private gate, David suggested that as an energy line (used by the Knights Templar centuries ago) went right through his rather large garden, we would all be welcome to meditate there and have a picnic afterwards.

As I'm not very good with dates it didn't strike me till a few hours later that the 12th August was the date of the group's third year together and that it was White Light Celebration time again. What a coincidence: I was bringing both sections of the group together to do some work for the Mother and we were going to eat, drink and be merry afterwards! We'd kill two birds with one stone! Tony had told me a few weeks prior that the 12th of August was important as far as the staff was concerned. Again, Tony knew nothing about the date of the White Light Celebration or that an Earth Healing Project was underway. This was being carefully supervised by the Masters. I really HAD to admit that now.

The information from Koot Hoomi began to pour in: Koot Hoomi himself would conduct the ceremony, with Jason Porthouse and Andy Thomas assisting me, overshadowed by Koot Hoomi, with the raising of the staff before Koot Hoomi placed it into the Heart Chakra. HE would give the Invocation. It was important that the staff must not touch the ground at any time before the ceremony or it would be more than useless; the staff would continue to be charged during the interim. After the ceremony the staff would be re-wrapped and buried by David Russell and group members Joy Byner and Molly Hegarty. It was to be placed east/west. Koot Hoomi's staff was an alchemical acupuncture needle, highly charged. It was the old magic/alchemy that closed down the higher courier lines and DNA strands, the ones that carried esoteric information, and it's the old magic that will revive them. But in time all this will be transformed anew as the Earth Mother's transformation takes place.

The staff remained wrapped in cloth and rested on my mother's oak table until the 12th August. The day before, on the 11th, I had left a container of water to be charged in the sun. It was now highly charged. On the morning of the 12th, I filled the little silver container with the water and put extra holy ash into the other silver bottle. All was prepared. Jason and Andy were due to pick me up at 10.50am. At 11 o'clock the phone rang: Andy had been held up in traffic, also it had begun to cloud over somewhat and a cold wind made its presence felt. If the negative forces were trying to thwart this ceremony then it had to be important and NOTHING was going to stop it, I'd make sure of that.

We finally arrived at Ashurst and entered David's house at about 11.45am. David, on Koot Hoomi's instructions, had created a six-pointed star on the lawn (the Seal of Solomon) and in the centre was the exact spot where the Heart Chakra courier line of the earth energy grid lay. It was this spot where the staff would be placed by Lord Koot Hoomi. I had also been asked by Koot Hoomi to invite a lady called Connie Link-Clark to the ceremony; I wasn't sure why, other than the fact that she had done so much work in networking information from the Masters of the Great White Brotherhood. I had no idea that Koot Hoomi was her master, nor did I know that she was to be the sixth person to participate in the ceremony. I thought it was I that made up the sixth. Wrong. You see, with the staff Tony had been inspired to make, there were six extra runes from the wood of the staff, one for each of the participants of the staff ritual.

Tony did not even know that six people were to be involved with the staff ceremony, he knew only that six runes were for six people, he did not know who. I had to dowse out which rune went to what person. The dowsing was some of the easiest that I've ever done: the dowsing rod went from rune to rune as swiftly as I called out the names: Molly, Joy, David, Andy, Jason. When I came to the last two runes, the rod told me which rune belonged to Jason, leaving one rune left which, obviously, I thought, had to be me. It was just after that, that Koot Hoomi asked me to contact Connie and invite her to be part of the ritual. My instructions were that I was to face north. David Russell was to be on the point of the star nearest to north, Molly was to stand to David's left and Joy to his right. To Molly's left, Jason was to stand and to Joy's right, Andy. The point of the star pointing due east was where Connie was to sit.

A beautiful 'OM' tape, of great intensity and beauty, had been composed by Keith, one of our members; he had also brought a wonderful sound system of excellent quality. The OM was tuned to the Heart Chakra (F natural). There were in all about 22 people. When everyone had taken their place in the garden around the star, Jason and Andy brought the staff to me. I knew they were going to have to help me/Koot Hoomi to place the staff in the exact spot and as the staff was eight foot tall I needed as much help as I could get. They unwrapped the staff and rested it across the arms of the chair I was sitting on.

After a few minutes, Koot Hoomi came through. He asked that the OM be sounded by all and that this would give the final charge to the staff. He instructed all those on the star as to their duties: at a given time He would ask Jason and Andy to raise the staff (being a polio person, my arms are weak). With His hands still grasping it, Koot Hoomi would then pull the staff down onto its spot, the Heart Chakra. Again, at a given time, He would call Molly to sprinkle the holy ash around the base of the staff as it stood on the earth. Then He would call Joy forward to sprinkle the holy water at its base. A very obvious alchemical process.

The OM began. I could feel the energy rising. My body began to shake and tremble slightly as it surged through me into the staff. Koot Hoomi raised the staff as high as my arms would permit. He then asked for Jason and Andy to step forward. They took the staff, turned it to the vertical, and positioned it over the small hole. Koot Hoomi pulled the staff down. He told Jason and Andy to return to their position. The energy was now pouring into the ground. Molly was called forward to sprinkle the holy ash and then Joy with the holy water. The ritual was at an end, but Koot Hoomi continued to hold the staff for minutes longer. Then he asked Keith to turn down the OM. He then thanked all those who had worked so hard to make this moment possible, especially Tony. He spoke of the great importance of what was taking place and that the staff was a final and necessary link in a vast chain of events, but that without the staff it would not have been possible. Then he said his farewells and was gone. I rounded off with a poem by the mystic Derek Neville.

Again, under Koot Hoomi's instructions, I left the burying of the staff to Molly, Joy and David. David had dug a trench on the east/west, aligned to true north with the head of the staff facing the rising sun. With everyone gathered around, it was like a small funeral, only this was a joyful one. The staff was given back to the Mother, cushioned with flowers.

The real significance of what had taken place was not known for two days. I knew that healing was now being poured into the Earth at a higher rate and that healers all over the planet would benefit also, their healing gifts going up a notch or three. The healing energy line that runs through David's house and garden doubled from 10 lines to 20. The main earth energy line that we had been working on went up four times from 10 to 40. This is not unusual when an energy line is being used. But the third and most significant part was yet to be revealed.

Meanwhile, the whole group had a party. Wonderful food was brought by each member of the group and Connie had a cake made in Koot Hoomi's honour. Many were moved to tears by the event and the sheer beauty of the occasion and some took a day or two to come down.

On the night of the following day, the information came through that what had been achieved was a raising of the earth courier lines from a ten line system to a twelve line system. Up until the 12th August, the number nine line was running at 47 per cent, the first eight lines were operating at 100 per cent and number ten line was in place but not activated. I dowsed that this information was correct then phoned Hilda Bell to check my findings. The next day I chased up Hilda, as I was anxious to know the result. Hilda confirmed that there was now a 12 line system in operation. Lines eleven and twelve were now in place, but not activated. She also told me that number nine line, currently running at 47 per cent, had risen greatly.

I had left a message on David Russell's answerphone to contact me and do a second check on these findings. Not only did David confirm, but he told me that number nine line was now running at 85 per cent and rising! But over and above that, number 10 line was now partially activated running at 0.5 per cent. The earth healing line, that connects every healer, hospital, healing sanctuary and sacred well on this planet had risen from 10 per cent to 28 per cent!

Lastly, Carole Coren, an old friend and psychic ally, received this information from her guide/teacher, Shomas, the evening before the ceremony:

"Today is the festival of Koot Hoomi. He is very excited that this is to happen. He is aware of the sacrifices people are making to be at this ceremony just for him and he is so pleased and grateful. It will be a happy time for you all. You will all raise the power of the energy lines and this in turn will raise the power of the whole grid. Ceremonies like this are

being performed all over the world in order to charge up the energy grid of the planet. The more energy, the higher the consciousness of the planet and all those upon her.

This is a great day, a glorious day in the life-time of Man – energies which have lain dormant for thousands of years are to be switched on like a light bulb. The power will be tremendous once it charges itself to full power. We are very happy this is happening today. There will be many more events like this over the next few years. It is needed desperately, it is part of a great network of energy running into the cosmos. Have a good day and thank you to all involved from us for the care and dedication they are putting into our work."

Koot Hoomi's Staff: after the ceremony.

EPILOGUE

*T*wo years after the staff ceremony, we moved to Anglesey, North Wales to be near my family. Just before that, I had been having trouble with my right hand. In fact, I couldn't even write my name properly.

I was giving a talk at the 1997 Glastonbury Crop Circle Symposium in Somerset and it was there that I started speaking gobbledegook (there are those amongst you who *still* feel that I'm talking, or writing gobbledegook!). It came out right in the end, but fellow lecturers, amongst them Michael Green, Andy Thomas and Michael Glickman – known to his friends as 'Glickers' - must surely have thought Bura had 'lost it' (how true that turned out to be). I thought at first that the old post-polio syndrome was again stalking me, trying to take yet another piece. I knew what I wanted to say, but it just came out wrong. I also knew that the words I was using to describe something were totally inadequate!

Then I had a 'fit' in my bed, and then another. The doctor was called and he in turn called the hospital in Bangor. I saw a neurologist by the name of Fletcher. My sister Josie went with me to see him. She had taken a few books that I had written (bless her) just to prove that I wasn't an idiot or going barmy! He didn't need to look at them because he suspected (by my symptoms) what it was. I was 'CD scanned' and Mr Fletcher's suspicions were confirmed. I had a brain tumour the size of an orange (as

Me, just as the effects of the tumour made themselves known. (Photo:- Hazel Leuchars.)

opposed to a *brain* the size of an orange?). The size of a Jaffa orange or the smaller Spanish variety, they didn't say. They removed it at The Walton Centre for Neurology and Neurosurgery, Liverpool. Being a meningioma-type tumour, it was considered benign, but I had to wait for 10 days for the lab to confirm it. It was benign.

I suffered a number of post-op infections. It was during the second infection when I was about to leave Bangor Hospital for my third journey to the Walton Centre to undergo yet more surgery to 'wash out' the infected flap in my skull that a certain gentleman phoned: "Hullo, this Uri Geller and I wish to speak to Paul Bura." It was a gentle but firm demand. Uri was a friend of my brother Kevin and his wife Maureen and directly he heard of my plight he phoned the hospital. The nurse, the familiarity of his name beginning to percolate in her mind, explained that I was very sick. "Why do you think I'm calling him?" Uri explained, as if it were obvious. "Please, I wish to speak to him." The nurse was taken off guard. Could this really be THE Uri Geller?

The last time I had any dealings with Uri Geller had been through the medium of television in the late '70s. I and thousands of others were hooked on his ability to apparently bend metal just by stroking it and sending out the thought: BEND! BEND! He conducted an experiment through our television screens. Of course, I sat with my forks and spoons in front of the screen whilst Uri conducted us with the words: BEND! BEND! He also claimed to mend broken watches: MEND! MEND! When it was all over and my spoons n' forks hadn't responded to the promptings of this slim, good looking young Jewish man, I happened to look up to a shelf on which stood a clock which had long since lost the will to live. I'm sure that it had two hands last time I looked at it. Now it had only one! I got up to examine the clock more closely and found that the large hand had fallen down in-between the glass front and the clock face. For some reason I turned the clock round to examine the back. The back was gradually being forced off! At my touch it suddenly sprang off, spewing cogs and wheels all over the floor!

Now Uri Geller was trying to talk to me and my nurse was perplexed. Perhaps she thought that all the surgical equipment in the hospital would either bend or malfunction? She gathered her thoughts and then said: "Well, he *is* in bed! Perhaps if you were to call back in 5 minutes?" "5 minutes? Okay, but do tell him Uri Geller wishes to speak to him." And he hung up. The nurse came to me and said: "There is a man on the phone and it sounds like Uri Geller. Do you want to speak to him? If so I'll push your bed to the phone?" I said, or rather stammered, as I was having trouble speaking, that I w-w-w-would l-l-like t-t-to sp-sp-speak to U-Uri Geller. The nurse wheeled me to the phone. Almost immediately the phone rang. It was Uri. The nurse handed the phone to me. "Uri?" I said. "Your brother Kevin explained your predicament and I wish to say to you that all will be well. You have to say to yourself 'all will be well' and MEAN it. Think positively and I will help you all I can." At that moment I filled with tears and instantly had a great love for this man who had simply picked up the phone, not knowing me from a hole-in-the-road. "You are filling with tears," he said prophetically, "no need to speak." I spluttered out a "Th-th-thank you." And he hung up.

They found the cause of my continued infection. The source was found to have come from the bone-flap itself... and they removed it.

I'm now into my seventh seven-year cycle. I said at the beginning of this book that the number 7 is *my* number, the number of *change*. Numerology, using my name and date of birth, confirms this. The tumour happened *completely out of sequence!* Now what does that say to you? It says to me, and I'm talking personally here, that the Earth is changing its frequency by the mere fact that the courier lines are no longer stuck on the number seven. Not because of what has happened to me (what arrogance, I hear you cry), that is a karmic symptom. What has happened in Kosovo and Yugoslavia; the shooting of school children in America; the nail bombings in London, are also a symptom, a karmic symptom. But the forces of negativity CANNOT WIN. Their backs are to the wall. When the changes that have been foretold will come, I've no idea and I don't pretend that I do. Time, in the cosmic sense, is difficult to predict, even though Joeb has told me that they will occur in and around 2012-2014. Perhaps, as has been said, they will come as a 'thief in the night'.

We live in a time-zone: we, all of us, want to do things more quickly, as if 'time' is the culprit, as if time is the enemy. Time is *not* the enemy, we are! The 'wake-up' call is echoing around the world (via the Courier lines that are hooked into our chakric system), the 'wake-up' call tells you who you really are.

Listen in silence for that cosmic alarm-clock for it will blow your mind!

Meanwhile, I shall continue to 'step to the drummer no matter how measured or far away.' My dream is one day to merge with the drummer and achieve Freedom itself. At the moment, I cannot even hold the sticks! Truth, Freedom, Love (the drummer), never changes. It's only our perception that changes.

What did I say at the beginning of this book? Oh yes:

COME IN NUMBER SEVEN, YOUR TIME IS UP!

About the Author

Paul Bura is a poet, writer and broadcaster.
He produced many of the voices behind
Thames Television's *Larry the Lamb*.
This was his first break and he subsequently
embarked on a career as a voice-over artist.
He went on to co-present Radio 4's
Sounds, Words and Movement and then moved
to Channel 4's *Same Difference* programme as
an on-screen reporter. He is a regular contributor
to magazines such as *The Science of Thought Review,*
The Quarterly and SC Magazine and co-wrote,
with Andy Thomas, *Quest for Contact.*

He is a performing poet:

"with a voice that would make
Dylan Thomas growl in his grave with envy":

thus said the writer and poet Christy Brown,
author of *My Left Foot* and *Down All The Days.*